45.⁰⁰

Summary of Contents

SEXY WEB DESIGN

BY ELLIOT JAY STOCKS

Sexy Web Design

by Elliot Jay Stocks

Copyright © 2009 SitePoint Pty. Ltd.

Expert Reviewer: Jina Bolton   **Editor**: Kelly Steele

Expert Reviewer: Dan Rubin   **Indexer**: Fred Brown

Managing Editor: Chris Wyness   **Cover Design**: Alex Walker

Technical Editor: Raena Jackson Armitage

Technical Director: Kevin Yank

Printing History:

First Edition: March 2009

Published by SitePoint Pty. Ltd.

48 Cambridge Street
Collingwood, Victoria, Australia 3066
Web: www.sitepoint.com
Email: business@sitepoint.com

ISBN 978–0–9804552–3–6
Printed and bound in Canada

About the Author

Always aspiring to create a unique look that's out of the ordinary, Elliot Jay Stocks's design is frequently featured in online and offline publications. His work is showcased on various design inspiration web sites, where it's used as an example of how accessible web design can still look beautiful. Elliot's portfolio includes Automattic, The Beatles, Blue Flavor, Twiistup, EMI Records, and Carsonified.

Elliot is also known to write about design trends, issues, and techniques for industry-leading publications such as *Practical Web Design* and *Computer Arts Projects*. He can be seen regularly at design conferences around the globe taking to the stage as both a speaker and a workshop host. Elliot's site can be found at http://elliotjaystocks.com/.

About the Expert Reviewers

Jina Bolton resides and works in San Francisco as an interaction designer at Crush + Lovely. Jina is a co-author of *The Art & Science of CSS* (Melbourne: SitePoint, 2007); she has also written articles for publications including *A List Apart*, *.net Magazine*, SitePoint, and Vitamin, and has spoken at conferences around the world. She enjoys traveling and learning Italian, and digs sushi and robots—and it's no coincidence that you'll find her website at http://sushiandrobots.com.

Dan Rubin is an accomplished user interface designer and usability consultant. He has over 10 years experience as a leader in the fields of web standards and usability. Dan is a sought-after public speaker and author, most recently penning *Pro CSS Techniques* (Berkeley: Apress, 2006) and *Web Standards Creativity* (Berkeley: friends of ED, 2007). He was an expert reviewer for *The Art & Science of CSS* (Melbourne: SitePoint, 2007), and blogs at http://superfluousbanter.org.

About the Technical Editor

Raena Jackson Armitage made her way to SitePoint via a circuitous route involving web development, training, and speaking. A lifelong Mac fangirl, she's written for *The Mac Observer* and *About This Particular Macintosh*. Raena likes knitting, reading, and riding her bike around Melbourne in search of the perfect all-day breakfast. Raena's personal web site is at http://raena.net.

About the Technical Director

As Technical Director for SitePoint, Kevin Yank oversees all of its technical publications—books, articles, newsletters, and blogs. He has written over 50 articles for SitePoint, but is best known for his book, *Build Your Own Database Driven Website Using PHP & MySQL*. Kevin lives in Melbourne, Australia, and enjoys performing improvised comedy theatre and flying light aircraft.

About SitePoint

SitePoint specializes in publishing fun, practical, and easy-to-understand content for web professionals. Visit http://www.sitepoint.com/ to access our books, newsletters, articles, and community forums.

To Samantha—partly for your patience, understanding, and support while I wrote evening after evening, but mostly because you're my source of happiness and inspiration!

To Mum and Dad—you nurtured my creativity from a very early age and you've always encouraged me at every step along the way.

To the citizens of the Internet—who would've thought a network of computers could allow me to meet so many great friends, travel the world, expose my work to millions of people, and indulge in my passion for art on a daily basis.

Table of Contents

Foreword

I like sexy things.

Now, hold on a moment—you can lower that eyebrow. I'm talking about objects that are beautiful and exciting—and that are quite removed from *sex*. I like it when I have a head-turning, jaw-dropping, breathtaking reaction from an item—whether it's a 1957 Corvette Stingray, a MacBook Air, or the elegant flourish of a beautiful typeface's ampersand. I'm talking about objects that are so well designed and downright stunning in both functionality and aesthetics that I stop and think, "Whoa—that's *sexy!*"

I'd like to just make one point clear. "Sexy" may be a four-letter word. But it's a *good* four-letter word. An item that's sexy is exciting. Appealing. Intriguing. Slick. It's an Eames lounge chair. It's that smokey bar jazz song. It's the upscale sushi lounge with soft, dim candle lights accompanied by the raspy, dramatic crooning of Portishead. Whatever it is that you find to be sexy, pay attention to it. Why do you find it sexy? Is it simply how it looks or is crafted? Is it how it works, too? Chances are, if you think an object is sexy, it's more than a pleasure to look at: it's a joy to use as well.

> "Whether you're designing a book, a software application, a piece of hardware, or a web site … think sexy."—Kathy Sierra

So, what about sexy web design? That is, after all, the title of this book. Well, the way I see it, sexy web design is all about the details—every intricate, delicate particular. When I see a web site that pairs great typography with a solid, well-designed grid, and makes use of stunning imagery and ornamentation, I just have to check it out. And as a designer for the Web, this is precisely the kind of reaction I want for my own work. That's where Mr. Stocks comes into play. Elliot is a consistent maker of objects that are sexy, when it comes to the Web.

In April of 2008, I was flown out to London for an unique opportunity: it was a live, onstage Photoshop battle for the Future of Web Design conference put together by Carsonified. The girl's team, consisting of Hannah Donovan (Creative Director at Last.fm) and myself, was against the boy's team of Jon Hicks (Hicksdesign) and none other than Elliot Jay Stocks. While I was certain that Hannah would totally rock this competition, I was a little nervous at the thought of being in a Photoshop battle against Elliot. Thankfully, my nerves were calmed a bit thanks to the Belgian beer that Elliot provided for the four of us during the contest.

But Elliot's great taste extends beyond beer. Look at his online portfolio; you'll see quite a range there—everything from gorgeous band and musician web sites to web industry-related conference sites; he's even produced print design work, iconography, and illustrations. Though his portfolio is diverse, throughout his body of work you'll find some common themes; elegant typography, interesting textures, and earthy, organic imagery are the ingredients that make up his recognizable style. These web sites are both visually beautiful, and user-friendly. Elliot has an attention to detail that inspires many web designers around the world, including myself. Oh yeah, it's sexy, too.

> "The visual image is a kind of tripwire for the emotions."—Diane Ackerman

If you're looking to begin creating sexy web sites yourself, then you're in luck. In this book, Elliot takes you through a holistic web interface design process. He helps you understand what interface design means, and he goes over the research needed to create a product that is of the highest quality. Then, he takes you through important layers in web design: the structure, interaction, and aesthetics. Finally, he gives tips for great design deliverables to ensure that the design is built and maintained properly. Again, it's all about attention to detail. Following Elliot's process, you'll create a great-looking, great-working web site … one you can call sexy.

I hope you're as excited as I am about this book. I feel so very fortunate to have been involved. It's the book I wish existed back when I was starting out in web design a decade ago. Watching this book grow and develop from concept to outline to draft reminds me of the very design process written about within these pages. There's a joy in watching an idea come to life. And when that web site or application idea becomes something beautiful and sexy—that's when joyful creation becomes a truly thrilling passion.

Jina Bolton

Preface

One of the great things about the Web is that virtually anyone can become a web designer: the tools are relatively cheap, the creation is instant, and the exposure is global. Of course, this is both a blessing and a curse, the title *designer* being brandished too easily in some instances. Web design is a craft, and creating a site that is truly beautiful, usable, and—most of all—enjoyable, requires skill, knowledge of design principles, and a mind open to exploring new techniques.

Who Should Read This Book?

What makes a web designer? Can a beginner with their first copy of Dreamweaver qualify? Or does it have to be an industry professional with an established reputation in design? The answer is both, and everyone in between. If you're responsible for the look, the feel, or the mood of a web site, you're a web designer—and this book is for you.

Whether you're completely new to web design, a seasoned pro looking for inspiration, or a developer wanting to improve your sites' aesthetics, there's something for everyone here. How? Because instead of trying to cover every possible area of creating a web site, I've focused purely on the design stage; that is, everything that happens before a single line of code is written.

However, great design is more than just aesthetics. Long before we open our graphics program of choice, we'll be conducting research, dealing with clients, responding to briefs, sketching out sitemaps, planning information architecture, moving from doodles to diagrams, exploring different ways of interactivity, and building upon design traditions.

But ultimately, we'll be finding out how to create web sites that look drop-dead *gorgeous*.

The SitePoint Forums

The SitePoint Forums[1] are discussion forums where you can ask questions about anything related to web design, development, hosting, and marketing. You may, of course, answer questions, too. That's how a discussion forum site works—some people ask, some people answer—and most people do a bit of both. Sharing your knowledge benefits others and strengthens the community. A lot of fun and experienced web designers and developers hang out there. It's a good way to learn new stuff, get questions answered in a hurry, and just have fun.

The Design Your Site forum[2] has sub-forums devoted to discussing tools, techniques, and even design critiques. It's free to sign up, and it takes just a few minutes.

---

[1] http://www.sitepoint.com/forums/
[2] http://www.sitepoint.com/forums/forumdisplay.php?f=40

This Book's Web Site

No book is perfect, and we expect that watchful readers will be able to spot at least one or two mistakes before the end of this one. The Errata page on the book's web site will always have the latest information about known typographical errors and updates. You'll find the book's web site at http://www.sitepoint.com/books/sexy1/. If you find a problem, you'll also be able to report it here.

The SitePoint Newsletters

In addition to books like this one, SitePoint publishes free email newsletters, such as *SitePoint Design View*, *SitePoint Market Watch*, and *SitePoint Tech Times*, to name a few. In them, you'll read about the latest news, product releases, trends, tips, and techniques for all aspects of web development. Sign up to one or more SitePoint newsletters at http://www.sitepoint.com/newsletter/.

Your Feedback

If you can't find an answer through the forums, or if you wish to contact us for any other reason, the best place to write is books@sitepoint.com. We have a well-staffed email support system set up to track your inquiries, and if our support team members are unable to answer your question, they'll send it straight to us. Suggestions for improvements, as well as notices of any mistakes you may find, are especially welcome.

Conventions Used in This Book

You'll notice that we've used certain typographic and layout styles throughout this book to signify different types of information. Look out for the following items:

Code Samples

Code in this book will be displayed using a fixed-width font, like so:

```
<h1>A Perfect Summer's Day</h1>
<p>It was a lovely day for a walk in the park. The birds
were singing and the kids were all back at school.</p>
```

If additional code is to be inserted into an existing example, the new code will be displayed in bold:

```
body {
  background: #336699;
}
```

A vertical ellipsis is used to highlight remarks inside the code examples:

```
<body>
  ⋮ This code remark doesn't need to be entered
</body>
```

Some lines of code are intended to be entered on one line, but we've had to wrap them because of page constraints. A ➥ indicates a line break that exists for formatting purposes only, and should be ignored.

```
background: #FFFFFF url("../resources/headers/logos/
➥banner-logo-600px.png") top left no-repeat;
```

Tips, Notes, and Warnings

Hey, You!

Tips will give you helpful little pointers.

Ahem, Excuse Me ...

Notes are useful asides that are related—but not critical—to the topic at hand. Think of them as extra tidbits of information.

Make Sure You Always ...

... pay attention to these important points.

Watch Out!

Warnings will highlight any gotchas that are likely to trip you up along the way.

Acknowledgements

Thanks to everyone at SitePoint for making this book possible and for asking me to write it in the first place—especially Raena, who kept me focused and inspired with her great ideas and insight.

Thanks to Jina and Dan for their expert reviews and for their continued friendship, even though they had to plough through my early drafts!

Thanks to the magazine editors, event organizers, clients, and employers of the world who've helped raise my profile to the extent where I'm being asked to write books. I'm honored.

Thanks to the talented designers working magic out there on the Internet; your wonderful work provides a constant source of inspiration, and has helped to make this book what it is.

And, as hinted at by the dedication message, thanks to my wonderful girlfriend, Samantha, who put up with me writing the book on many a long evening, and gave me huge amounts of support, praise, and cups of tea.

Chapter 1

Interfaces are Sexy

I'm going to be honest. The reason I'm a designer is a simple one:

I like making stuff look pretty.

There, I said it. You know my secret. I've laid myself bare and that's a fair way to start a book.

But web design goes beyond making things look pretty. It's also about making them *work*. Rather than just concocting passive visuals, web designers create **interfaces**, systems that allow a person to interact with an object or system to achieve a goal. The best web designs give clear visual signals on how to go about the task.

Web sites—by their very nature—are all interfaces, even though some look more like plain, practical tools; think of the clean form design from 37signals' online tools, shown in Figure 1.1. Others—like the more complex Future of Web Apps Miami 2008 site,[1] shown in Figure 1.2—are more decorative.

---

[1] Unfortunately, this site is no longer online.

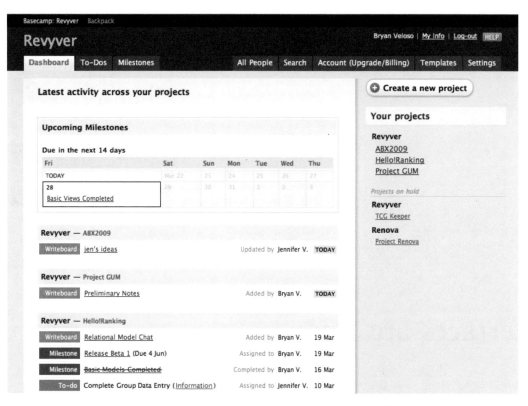

Figure 1.1. The clean, simple interface of 37signals' Basecamp[2]

Figure 1.2. The 2008 Future of Web Apps Miami

---

[2] http://www.basecamphq.com/

So what are we hoping to achieve when we design a web site? Well, my aim is to create an interface that people find genuinely enjoyable to use. And although a web site—by its interactive nature—has to be *used*, I'm also interested in how it's *viewed*. After all, we're web designers, so we need to concentrate on the look. Functionality will form a significant part of the book—but the main focus will be on creating interfaces that look great while engaging the user.

Interfaces

Interfaces are all around us, and once you know how to spot one, you'll start to see them everywhere.

Think of you—the user—and an object that you need to control, or a goal that you want to achieve. In between the object and ourselves we have the interface: a simple method of achieving our goal. Although it's not true to say that an interface is always simple, it's true that an interface's role is to simplify a task.

Users are People Too!

By the way, while we're sitting here comfortably, right at the beginning of the book, let me add a brief note on the term *user*. It's one that fails to particularly appeal to me, given how it seems so tech-centric. Keep in mind that a user is simply a human being, an average Joe, a passerby on the street who might be a web-savvy tech-support guru, or an elderly lady who's only just started using a computer. People *use* web sites, so it's a handy term, but just try to keep in mind that we're talking about regular humans, rather than some kind of machine-operating robot.

Interfaces in the Real World

Before we leap on to the Web, let's think about interfaces around us in the real world. This will help to coax us into the habit of analyzing the processes of interaction. We'll start with a simple example: a plug. (Oh, and I wholeheartedly confess that I started with a plug because it was the first thing I saw when I looked up from my screen.) Figure 1.3 shows us an everyday UK wall plug.

It can be helpful to break an interaction apart into its components: the user (this can be an object), the interface itself, feedback, and the goal.

User	Interface	Goal	Feedback
Laptop plug	On and off switch on the wall	Socket connected to mains power	On indicator

I click the switch down, electricity surges through the cable to my laptop, and I'm able to carry on writing for another hour. Lucky me!

But the role of the interface goes beyond simplifying the task in hand—it should also give us information about whether the task has or hasn't been completed: **feedback**. In the UK, our wall sockets usually have a little red indicator which appears when the power is turned on; you can see this in Figure 1.3. Therefore, I know I've achieved my *goal* (if it's not too big a term to call it that) because of the feedback provided by the indicator on the top of the depressed switch.

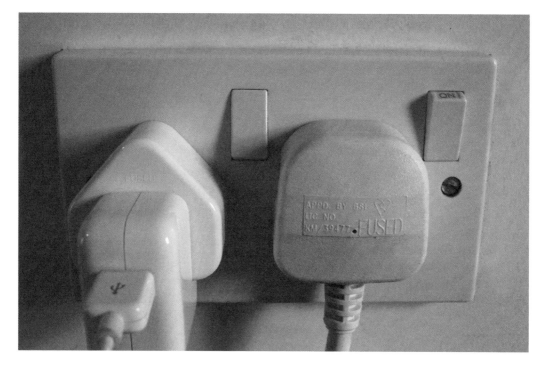

Figure 1.3. The ON indicator shows me it's on.

Let's take another example: a digital camera, like the one shown in Figure 1.4. When we're about to take a photo, there's a bit more going on here in terms of interface. In fact, I'd say that my camera's interface is built up of three mini interfaces:

- the function buttons on the hardware, which allow me to change the settings
- the LCD screen, which provides me with information on the camera's settings
- the shutter button, which is clickable, and provides me with audible feedback when I press it

Yet this more complex, layered interface still fits neatly into our system:

User	Interface	Goal	Feedback
Me	Function buttons + LCD screen + shutter	A photo	Sounds + visual indicators; the photo is displayed

Figure 1.4. Your standard digital camera (Photo: Canon)

Interfaces on the Web

Now that we know how to break down an interaction into its parts, let's look at some interactions on the Web.

Imagine a form, like the one shown in Figure 1.5. You want the user to fill in your form, but you don't want them to submit it without filling in the required fields. What's more, you want to show and hide certain fields depending on what they input (for example, if someone answers that they have a car, you might want to show a drop-down menu that lists car manufacturers). The form interface provides us with feedback in the guise of a message or indicator.

User	Interface	Goal	Feedback
Me	Required form fields + Optional form fields + Submit button	Form submission	Submission message

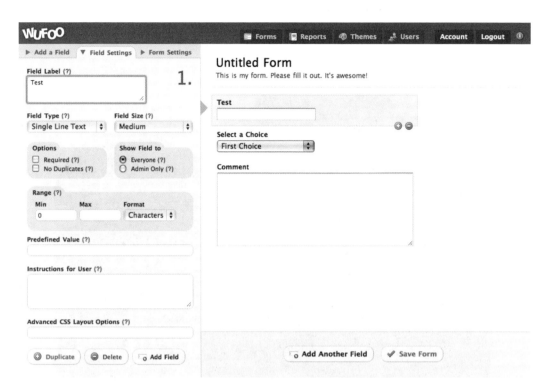

Figure 1.5. A form in action

It's not all about bare-bones functionality, though. Remember: this book is about *sexy* web design, so we'll be looking at ways to build interfaces that are stunning as well as useful.

Web Design Goals

Let's face it, the Web is often a fairly barren landscape: just think of its dull, text-based roots. In many respects, progress has been limited in the short time that's passed since the Web's conception. Web technologies have evolved and improved, but they've hardly been radical changes; the core elements of HTML are still at the heart of what we do, and as such there are myriad constraints in which we have to work. Even if you forget design centered on web standards and consider Flash, factors such as the limited **viewport**, or screen size, variable connection speeds, and restricted hardware capabilities suggest there's major scope for improvement.

Like all goals, successful and engaging web design is as much about overcoming technical challenges as it is about creating an attractive product. But technicalities shouldn't hinder you from achieving your goal: to create a site that's a joy to behold.

What Your Site Does

Web site designs are often presented as static images in the design stage, but by their very nature undergo a transformation by the time the project is completed. So when we're designing with static images, we need to stay mindful of *how* that image will eventually work within a web site.

This sobering thought also reminds us that we should hold off from firing up Photoshop for a moment and invest some time into the logic behind our web site. I'm not talking about logic in a technical, code-heavy sense; just that we should consider the processes involved in using a web site. At its basic level, that means questions like: "What is the major call to action for this site? What do we want the user to *do*?" At the other end of the spectrum, we have factors such as where to place elements or which photo to use.

How Your Site Looks

Let's establish one standard rule here:

The more attractive an item looks, the longer people will want to look at it.

Yes, that's right: design an appealing-looking website and users are more likely to receive your client's message, buy their product, engage in their community, or do what you want them to do. What's more, they'll return, like I often do to the beautiful Fall For Tennessee[3] site shown in Figure 1.6. Now, there's a reason to care about great design (and probably more valid than my "I like to make stuff look pretty" mantra).

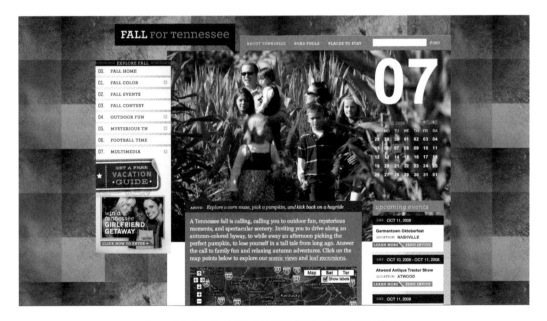

Figure 1.6. The absolutely beautiful Fall For Tennessee web site

---

[3] http://fall.tnvacation.com/

Usability and Accessibility

With the Internet allowing our work to reach a global audience, we have to try and cater for a massive range of people: blind users, elderly users, underage users, users with slow Internet connections or older, unreliable machines, users with little knowledge of the way web sites work, technology enthusiasts who expect nothing short of cutting edge … the whole spectrum.

While part of a web site's accessibility depends on the markup, quite a lot of it is governed by the design. Throughout the book, we'll be taking both accessibility and usability into consideration throughout the design phase. If you keep your users in mind at all times, then the road to usability nirvana will be an easy one.

Design Process

Like the creation of any successful artifact, a web site needs to *evolve*. It involves planning and preparation, and takes shape over a period of time. The more planning and forward-thinking we can do as designers, the better. Preparation helps us sort a project into nice, neat, orderly piles—defining specific goals along the way—and assists in foreseeing any potential problems that could set us back. In general, it's safe to say that planning out the site's creation process in detail makes everyone's lives easier. Happy designers. Happy developers. Happy clients. All of them happy people, if not slightly shiny.

Research

Research is a stage that's often misunderstood and often overlooked. When a project's budget is tight, the research phase is almost certainly one of the victims, usually because it's less tangible than the stages that make up the finished product. But it does still make up the final product! Without research, we're flying blind: we're jumping straight into the creative process without fully understanding the context in which we're creating.

If you're feeling a little daunted by this research concept, relax. It's a stage that only needs to use up a small amount of time, and a lot of the preliminary client and designer discussions that happen all fall under the umbrella of research.

The most common form research takes is asking the client to name web sites that he or she likes and dislikes. Questioning the client further, asking why they like or dislike those web sites—or elements of those sites—is even more helpful. In fact, in many instances, I've even found this to be as informative as a design brief! If the client can then explain how those preferences relate to their own brand values that they're trying to portray—or the functionality they want their own customers to experience—then you have a design brief right there.

In truth, research is a bit of a vague term, but this is a good state of affairs: the kind of research you do depends on the type of project you're working on. I'm going to suggest a few different methods of research that you can apply to your projects, but they're all interchangeable. Keep it loose, keep your mind open, and prepare for the project in any way that feels natural and helpful to you, your colleagues, and your client.

Structure

With our research complete, and a collection of sources of guidance and inspiration, it's time to start planning. But where do we start?

Stay away from that computer! Seriously—go and sit away from a computer (there are such places), get some paper and a pen, and start scribbling.

The structure of a site should come freely, with as little restraint as possible. In the beginning, keep it loose, and approach the task without being encumbered by exact technical concerns. They're worth considering, it's true, but the decisions at this stage should be based on what the site can become—rather than worrying about how specific form elements should be displayed. Figure 1.7 shows you one of my very rough, early diagrams.

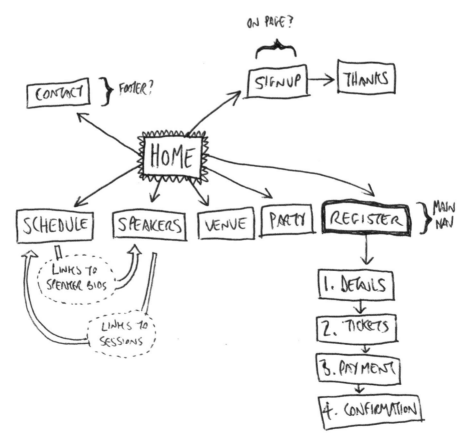

Figure 1.7. Very rough!

Information Architecture

As the plan for the site gradually evolves, you can begin focusing on certain areas. What should be the key message that hits the user when the site loads? What is the primary call to action? How many pages should there be? What should be on each page? What elements should be on all pages? How does each element relate to the goals of the web site? Each of these questions relate to **information architecture**; in terms of the Web, this is the science of organizing information in a useful and logical manner.

There are debates about how much of this we should do as designers, and indeed, Information Architecture is often a job in itself. However, as so many projects require us designers to pick up some of the reins of an information architect, it's important that we get a grounding in the practice.

Wireframing

In my wild, heady days of web design youthfulness, I regularly made the mistake of starting a site design by jumping straight into Photoshop. In my defense, this was a case of the circumstances at hand: the company I was working for at the time often sprang projects on us that had almost no time frame. The brief arrived in the morning and they needed the site live by the evening … of the previous day. But whereas some of these turned out to be relatively successful web sites, I would recommend that you first draw up decent **wireframes**—blueprints for your design—on paper before heading straight into creating full-blown designs. Sure, you can use Photoshop to create your wireframes, like the one in Figure 1.8—in fact, you can use any tool you wish—but I'd recommend starting off with good ol' fashioned pen and paper.

In the Wireframing section of Chapter 2, I'll take you through a variety of techniques, starting with pen and paper, and finishing with some neat, computer-generated diagrams, ready to form the basis of your actual designs.

We'll be using Photoshop to create these, but if you'd rather use another application like Fireworks or OmniGraffle, that's fine—choose whichever production process best suits your workflow!

Figure 1.8. Wireframes start to take shape

Tone, Mood, and Atmosphere

Rounded corners and gradients might look great on some sites, but terrible on others. Your messy, grungy background image might sit well on a site for a heavy metal band, compared to, say, a dental practice. So we'll be exploring the various moods and atmospheres we can create using changes in visual style. We'll look at what approaches to take, when to use them, and when to use alternatives.

On any web site, the goal of the visual style is to evoke a feeling in the end user—a feeling that ties in with the concepts and values of the company (or individual) the site is trying to promote. And because we're dealing with imagery rather than words, our job is to convey that atmosphere in an almost subliminal manner. For example, the imagery used in the design for the Dara's Garden[4] site, shown in Figure 1.9, creates an atmosphere of relaxed elegance.

Figure 1.9. The relaxed and elegant site for Dara's Garden

Interaction

There's very little you can do on a web site without involving some form of interaction. Reading through information still involves scrolling through the text, and fairly much everything above that involves interaction on a more complex scale: pushing buttons, submitting search queries, opening menus, navigating through multiple pages … the simple act of visiting a web site invariably means that you'll be engaging in an interactive experience.

Navigation

What's the most important thing on a web site? Well, the content, I suppose. But the content needs to be found, and here the user is aided in that most complex of missions by navigation elements. In this sense, then, the navigation is the most important *interactive* element of any web site.

Navigation comes in many forms. The visual style applied to navigation can signify a type, as well as demonstrate a hierarchy to the user; and that hierarchy could be within the navigation itself, or how it relates to other navigational forms on the page. We'll look at different navigation styles in detail, such as hyperlinks, menus that collapse and expand, drop-down menus like the kind you'd find in your operating system, lists of pages, tabs—all helpful devices in guiding a user effectively

---

[4] http://www.darasgarden.com/

around your web site. You can see a variety of navigation styles being used on Erratic Wisdom[5] in Figure 1.10.

Figure 1.10. A variety of navigation styles on the Erratic Wisdom web site

Forms

Forms can be extremely tedious to style, but taking the time to apply some polish so they look right—like Mint,[6] shown in Figure 1.11— can really make the difference between a slapdash job and a great design. It's more than about changing the colors to match your site's palette; aspects such as aligning input fields' widths and positions to the grid can allow the user to scan through the form elements and find out how best to fill in the information. Taking inspiration from some of the best examples on the Web, we'll design forms that use inline messages to give extra information to the user, guiding them through the form completion process. We'll look at everything from the humble search form, to the newsletter sign-up, right through to the registration process on a more complex web application.

---

[5] http://erraticwisdom.com/
[6] http://www.haveamint.com/

Figure 1.11. The preferences panel inside Mint illustrates the attention given to creating great-looking forms

Audio and Video

With the popularity of sites like YouTube[7] and MySpace,[8] audio and video players have become commonplace on the Web. Although often restricted by the interaction systems they've inherited from offline media, we'll look at how these can work very effectively. We'll also try to maximize the potential of these particular interfaces: how to make them as unobtrusive as possible and let the media speak for itself. The video player interface used on the Vimeo[9] site is shown in Figure 1.12.

---

[7] http://youtube.com/
[8] http://myspace.com/
[9] http://www.vimeo.com/

Figure 1.12. The minimal but informative interface on the Vimeo player

Desktop Behavior

In the grand scheme of things, computers have only been around for a minimal time. But the Web's been around for an even shorter period, so most of our web interface basics have been inherited from the desktop applications to which we've become accustomed. As web applications become more complex, we're finding online experiences that closely resemble desktop behavior: dragging and dropping, image viewing and manipulation, and—in the case of web sites at the cutting-edge—experiences that don't even feel like they're happening inside a browser. The interface of the 280 Slides[10] web site, shown in Figure 1.13, looks and feels just like the desktop application as Microsoft PowerPoint.

---

[10] http://www.280slides.com/

Figure 1.13. A desktop-like experience in the browser from 280 Slides

Aesthetics

Let's face it: this is the fun part. You've planned your project, prepared your research, sorted out your wireframes and information architecture … now it's time to crack open the tins of paint and start throwing colors at the canvas, Jackson Pollock style![11]

Not only is this phase the most satisfying to every designer's *inner artist*, but we really can relax a little and have some fun; we've planned everything up to this point so that we have a clear idea of the framework on which we can work our design magic. I must admit that I've sometimes been a little too eager to jump into fully-fledged Photoshop mockups without doing the groundwork. But it's definitely worth the wait!

Layout and Composition

People talk about web design as a young medium, and while in many senses that's true, they're disregarding the immense history of design practices that the new mode inherits; hence, the key principles of web design are exactly the same as those of print. Traditional graphic design concepts such as layout, typography, and color theory remain just as relevant on the Web; all that's changed is the constraints under which we work. In Figure 1.14, we can see how the Volunteer Lawn site[12] packs in plenty of information without becoming overwhelming or cluttered.

---

[11] Jackson Pollock is an artist known for his technique of splattering color in big, bold strokes. Thankfully, Photoshop is less prone to causing a mess on your studio floor.

[12] http://www.vollawn.com/

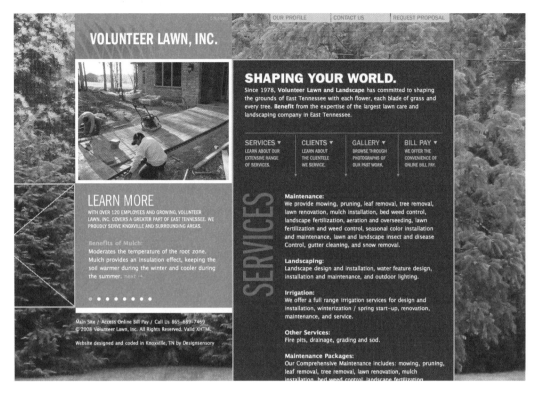

Figure 1.14. Volunteer Lawn's site layout has lots to see without getting lost amidst clutter

One key difference between design for print and design for the Web is the nature of the medium. A printed brochure has fixed dimensions, and every copy looks exactly alike. For the Web, the dimensions and layouts can vary—for example, the size of the browser window or the capabilities of the device they're using—and the possible combinations are different for every user. Are they viewing the site on a 30-inch Apple Cinema Display or a mobile phone? What fonts do they have on their system? Are they running the latest version of the Flash Player? Can the user even see the web site, or are they relying on a screen reader to convey the site's content?

The truth is we're unable to control exactly how our web site is experienced, and this point is reinforced to me every time I embark on a new project. But rather than treat this as an obstacle, we should embrace this flexibility as the chance to use the medium to its full advantage. After all, my grandmother is unable to increase the font size on her local paper, but she can enlarge it on her newspaper's web site. Working on the Web is our chance to serve up content flexibly, in a way best suited to our users.

A Change of Scenery

Designing for all kinds of different displays and capabilities can be quite a challenge. If you need some respite, I heartily recommend that you do some print design every now and then. Compared with designing for the Web, the predictability of a paper object is a very welcome break—plus you'll get the chance to learn some of the skills specific to designing for print!

The Artistic Layer

Here's another unfortunate truth: a lot of people see what web designers do as utterly pointless. Why bother creating a seamlessly repeating, background-image texture when you could have a flat color? Why add a subtle shadow beneath your content boxes when a simple 1-pixel border will do? Well, because we know how much difference it can make! That's one of my main passions when it comes to design: adding that extra touch of TLC to a project can really improve a site's look, regardless of how subtle it is. Attention to detail goes a long way towards creating a visually rewarding experience for people: it can be the distinction between good and great design. Figure 1.15 illustrates small embellishments on the Decor8 site[13], such as the fabric patterns, stitched motif, and the neat display of a range of information. It really is that subtle!

Figure 1.15. Lots of visually pleasing enhancements on the Decor8 site

We're going to explore how we can apply these little touches to our web sites. How does your choice of color reflect the message you're trying to convey? How can we evoke the right atmosphere with our design? Let's consider how Art principles—yes, with a capital A—influence design. We're going to give designs soul, personality, and character!

Most importantly, you're going to see how it's possible for these artistic ideals to sit alongside web-centric concepts like functionality and usability. At times it's inevitable that the two must compete, but we'll be striving for the common ground. We'll be looking at how contrast can improve legibility, how color and pattern can form consistency, and how mood and tone can be set through careful attention to the details.

---

[13] http://decor8blog.com/

Typography

In recent times, typography on the Web has developed a bit of a cult following, having been largely ignored by designers in the Web's formative years. Sites such as I Love Typography[14] are at the forefront of this reinvigorated interest in the art form, and designers like Jason Santa Maria, whose site you can see in Figure 1.16, are leading the pack with experiments in type.

Relatively new techniques—such as image replacement, Flash text replacement, and CSS3's improved support for including typefaces in your style sheets—are slowly opening up more methods for displaying type on the Web. We'll be exploring some of the tricks we can use in our design to create fantastic effects, as well as what we can achieve with the most common, *web-safe* fonts for great-looking type. Here we'll examine traditional typographic techniques that are easy to implement, yet can help spice up some ordinary text. But rest assured, our focus extends beyond usability; there's room for experimentation here, and I intend to use it. Because believe it or not, the concepts of sexy type and accessible text aren't necessarily mutually exclusive!

And why stop there? Let's look at the exciting artifacts that have been produced by print designers and see how far we can take those on the Web.

Figure 1.16. Jason Santa Maria's[15] continually changing use of bold typography

Images

It's possible to achieve great design on the Web without the use of any imagery: well-structured grids, mindful use of color, and typographic treatments can be enough to create a beautiful look without an image in sight. However, imagery does play a key role in conveying a sense of atmosphere.

An image can take many forms: a photograph of a person for an *About* page, or an illustrative diagram to explain a concept on a blog post—these kind of images add visual *value* to content. But then there's the **presentational**, or decorative aspect: for instance, an image might simply be a box shadow or a rounded corner—the kind of thing that enhances the visual styling of the page. Since this is a book about design, presentational images will be our main focus.

---

[14] http://ilovetypography.com/
[15] http://jasonsantamaria.com/

Another example of imagery used frequently in web design is, of course, **iconography**. In a way, iconography is a combination of content and presentation: it adds meaning to content while dressing it up in a visually pleasing manner.

Given that so much of a web site's visual style can be controlled by imagery, and because images can be broken down into so many subgroups that perform different functions, we'll be spending a significant amount of time in this area of web design.

Convention versus Innovation

You know what really winds me up? Boring web sites. No, hang on—that's wrong. What really winds me up are web designers who settle for the mundane, rather than attempt an uncommon path. It really is easy to design a great-looking web site that incorporates a few bold, original elements to set it apart from the crowd. I'm going to show you how having a little bit of courage to be different—despite how small—can really go a long way.

Figure 1.17. Some bold use of whitespace on the Revyver site[16]

It's more than just about breaking the mold, though; after all, conventions are there for a reason. While innovation helps to push things forward and move trends along, convention provides a framework of proven concepts that work; that is; systems that people recognize. A simple example is how we almost always place our navigation in a strip near the top of the page, or to the left or right of the content. These are conventions that work, and in this instance they work because it ensures the navigation appears in the area of the screen that the user will see first.

---

[16] http://www.revyver.com/

Drop-down form elements are a traditional way of displaying price ranges (such as $10–$20, $21–$50, and so on), but the Kayak site, pictured in Figure 1.18, opted for draggable sliders to filter their search results instead. A slider is still a convention (more from the desktop than the Web), but using it in this sense gives the site visitor a visual way of customizing their results. It's an interesting example of how a convention—used in a new way—can actually become an innovation.

Figure 1.18. Instead of using drop-down menus for price filtering, Kayak uses draggable sliders[17]

Deliverables

So you've designed the best-looking web site in the world and you're shopping for the suit or gown you'll be wearing to the celebrity-packed design awards ceremony that you just *know* you'll be invited to. But hang on a minute—your site needs to be built first!

The good news is that, although web site building is beyond the scope of this title, there are already several wonderful books on the subject (with many published by SitePoint, of course!) that will guide you on your way to development enlightenment. So, you're covered, whether your tastes favor front-end code like HTML, CSS, or JavaScript, or server-side heavy stuff like PHP, Rails, or—yikes—.NET. Brave you.

But you and I aren't getting off that lightly, and if I'm going down, I'm taking you with me. So, last but by no means least, we're going to look at **deliverables**—that is, how to split your lovely Photoshop output into individual image files, ready for a developer to build. It's not all slicing and dicing, though. Imagery needs to be prepared with its final context in mind, so that a great design concept can still look sensational when recreated on an actual web page.

On a personal note, I'm usually responsible for the front-end code (such as HTML, JavaScript, and CSS) as well as the design itself, so I always have the production stage in mind right from when the design begins. This is an advantage I believe every web designer should possess, regardless of whether they're responsible for code. For this reason, you'll notice that every example in this book

---

[17] http://www.kayak.co.uk/

is created with that consideration in mind. The appearance and usability of the end result should remain paramount in the designer's head: substance should never be sacrificed for style.

Design Comps

When you finish designing a web site and prepare for its development phase—whether it's to be handled by you or another developer—what exactly is it you hand over? Your final design **comp**—short for comprehensive artwork—is your completed design, ready for a developer to build. I'll be looking at the best way to present your static designs using a simple guide to best practices. But before we even get to the finished stage, we'll be exploring ways of showcasing your ideas to the client as the design progresses. In essence, we'll be getting down and dirty with how to handle all these files flying back and forth.

Figure 1.19. Part of our finalized design comp

Style Guides

It's not just files, though. Often it's useful—and sometimes essential—that we hand over style guides along with the finished design. Style guides are also associated with brand, identity, and logo design, and are used to ensure that the brand is carried across all of the paraphernalia produced by a business, but they're equally important in web design. Mostly, this is because you might be handing over the design to a third party who'll actually be building the site—but on web sites where there are thousands of pages generated dynamically, style guides are like page templates: indications of how certain sections of the design can be applied to a page, regardless of the variable content.

When it comes to interaction, style guides can also help describe a non-visual process. For instance, "when we click an X type of button, an X type of box should always appear before the page reloads."

And be assured: style guides are useful for you *as well as* other people. You may find you have to return to a job several months after completion, only to find that you've forgotten how things should look and work!

Let's Start Working

So as you can see, we're going to be covering the entire design process in this book: from initial ideas through to when we finally hand it over. Along the way we're going to look at best practices, knowing the rules and when to break them, and how to create absolutely beautiful web sites.

Follow me, if you will, on the road to—drumroll, please—sexy web design!

Research

Before we decide *how* we're going to create our design, we need to decide *what* it is we're going to create. Well, that's easy—the client just gives us a design brief, and then we get to work—right?

Well, you could do that, but you'd be missing out on the all-important research stage. Fortunately, we've got a whole chapter devoted to just that.

The Brief

A **design brief** details what the client expects of the design you'll build. A brief is an understanding between client and designer, rather than a formal document denoting a contract between two parties. And the better you understand each other, the more likely the outcome will make both parties proud. Most importantly, the more detailed the brief (even if it takes the form of several email, phone, or face-to-face conversations back and forth), the more chance you have of fulfilling its requirements. In other words, *brief* is a totally inappropriate term!

Imagine you receive a note like this:

> Dear web designer,
>
> I'd like a web site, please. I want it to look really cool and stylish! It should be really fun and easy to use.

A brief as basic as this is unhelpful. What does it tell us? Absolutely nothing! Every client wants a web site that looks cool and stylish, and is fun and easy to use. I'm still waiting for the day when a client asks me for a site that looks utterly terrible and fails to work. Now that'd be an interesting brief!

Guiding a Brief

To receive a detailed brief from our client, we should help them out a little. Remember, some people can do with a bit of help in putting a brief together.

Kick things off by asking questions. Giving your client a set of focused, direct questions should result in quality answers. Vague, open-ended questions begets nebulous answers—that is, nothing useful!

Some Basic Questions

The questions you ask will really depend on the kind of site you're building, but there are some basic questions that are useful for any project:

- What do you want someone to do once they've visited your site—that is, what is the **call to action**?
- How should a user feel when they visit your site, and what should be their lasting experience?
- Name three sites that appeal to you and explain what it is you like about them.
- Name three sites you don't like and explain why you dislike them.
- What is your budget and ideal time frame?

These questions are important, because you'll instantly find out some practical guides for the design you'll create, such as:

- the business goal behind the site
- the intended emotional effect
- what you could possibly emulate
- what you should definitely avoid being influenced by
- how much time you can spend

Many companies or individuals won't understand the concepts you take for granted as a tech-savvy web geek. Try to guide them through the process using everyday language, and only introduce a technical term when you can explain what it means and why they should take interest in it.

Working with an Established Framework

You might find that your client already has a strong idea about what they expect from the design, especially if they're a larger company. They may have specific guidelines or requirements based on organizational policy, or they may have already sought recommendations from other web professionals, such as information architects or usability consultants. Larger projects might involve more in-depth research into the target audience; this could take the form of user-testing on existing web sites with the creation of **user personas**—character sketches of typical visitors to your site—as a guide to your site's future audience. In this book we're concentrating mostly on smaller projects, so these kinds of situations are beyond the scope of our example project—but if you find yourself in this situation, naturally it will form part of the brief, and you'll need to take these requirements into account.

Expanding the Brief

Imagine our client sends an email containing the following brief, based on the five questions we asked them:

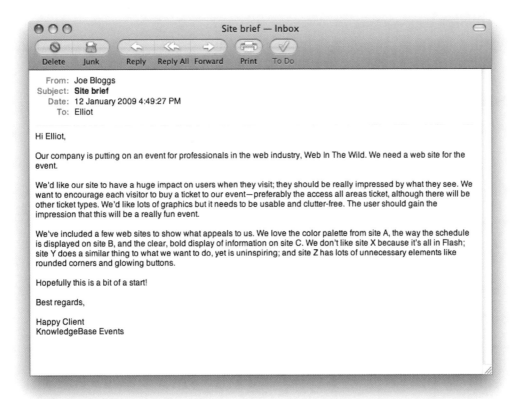

As briefs go, that's a fairly informative one—there's plenty of detail—yet it also gives us lots of scope to be inventive. Let's have a look at what we can take from it.

What Has the Brief Told Us?

- main goal: buy *access all areas* ticket
- look: visually rich, clear and uncluttered, an atypical style with a big impact
- feel: fun; the *access all areas* ticket title alludes to a VIP pass at a gig
- technology: not keen on Flash

What Do We Still Need to Find Out?

- We know that the primary goal of this site is to encourage the visitors to buy tickets, but can the client also define any additional goals?
- Are they entirely against the use of Flash, or are they happy to use it where the site would most benefit?
- Apart from ticket sales, what's the main information the site should convey about the event?
- In terms of visual style, what are they looking for? Are they after a design aesthetic in particular?
- How soon is *as soon as possible*? (This is irrelevant to us in our fictional situation, but it certainly would matter in the real world!)

As hypothetical as this is, you can still see that some answers have the tendency to create more questions. This is good, though: it's all part of the process, and more questions help you to refine the brief.

The Finalized Brief

After some more discussion with the client regarding these questions, we can add more detail to our brief.

It's worth noting that our client has given us some technical information, such as the use of Flash and fixed widths, but it's unlikely that most clients will be that web-savvy. Remember, hold your client's hand when required. It's probably unnecessary for you to explain every last decision to them, but try to answer any questions they might have. For instance, if they're adamant that *all* text should be resizable, be sure to explain to them that image-based text is unable to be resized as cleanly as normal text.

Project Desirables

- The main objective is to encourage the user to buy an *access all areas* ticket.
- The secondary objective is for the user to buy another ticket type.
- A general objective is to generate interest in the event.
- Information should be immediately obvious and clearly displayed.
- A balance should be struck between a *fun* atmosphere and a sense of authority and expertise, provided by the big-name speakers.

Technical Requirements

- The design can be of a fixed width.
- Top-level navigation will remain the same across each page, but there will be various sub-menus that change depending on where you are.
- JavaScript may be employed for an enhanced user experience.
- Flash can be used in moderation, but only for small parts of the site. All key elements (such as the navigation and main content) should be rendered in HTML.
- Images may only be used for h1 and h2 headings; h3 and lower will be text.
- Advertising will be used on the site (sparingly) in the form of sponsor logos, so space should be reserved for it.

First Steps

Let's begin with the first logical step. We're going to be creating a web site for an event, so we need to analyze the **brand values** associated with the event: these in turn will be the core concepts that the site needs to convey. Let's imagine we ask our client for some brand values, and they give us the following ideas to work with:

- fun and exciting: more than just a conference
- credibility: advice from the absolute experts
- inventive and innovative: a group of creative people open to new ideas

Already that might start conjuring up some stylistic ideas in our minds, but let's leave that for the moment. We should be asking ourselves: what makes up an event site? Our client has yet to specify the actual pages they want, so we'll help them out by brainstorming:

- Home: an introduction to the event; leads people into other parts of the site
- Bookings: to sell the ticket types
- Schedule: for details about the event
- Speakers: an easy glance at the experts involved
- Venue: where the event is located and the facilities available
- Sponsors: may appear in the sidebar or footer, rather than a page of its own
- Community: parties, links to social networks, photos, and so on

Let's take a look some of the values we want to convey with our site, and take a peek at how other event web sites go about it.

The Element of Fun

Events—or, more specifically, the kind we like to have in the web community—tend to emphasize the convivial aspect. Who would've thought that people like to hang out with their friends and colleagues for a social drink?

With the fun element being such an important selling point, it makes sense for us to give this a lot of prominence on our web site. Although it's important to stress the knowledge that can be gained at such events, we all know that we're *just as* interested in the parties! That's why we'll suggest to our client that a whole page should be dedicated to social gatherings happening around the event, with the imagery of the site portraying a fun, party-like atmosphere.

Gravitas and Authority

But we mustn't get carried away with all this *fun* malarkey. We need to make it clear that this is a credible, serious event, too. Otherwise, how else are delegates going to convince their bosses to pay for this out of their training budget? The web site for Web Directions North, shown in Figure 2.1, is neat, clean, and means business.

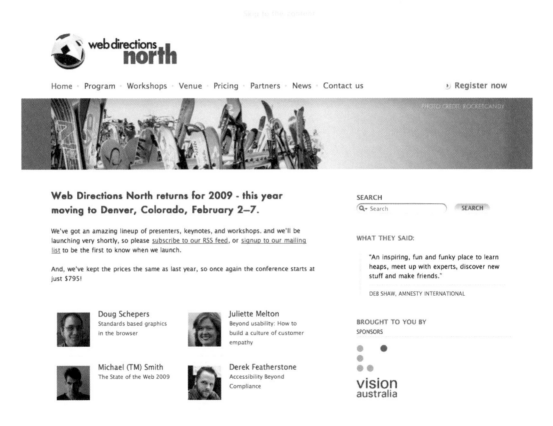

Figure 2.1. The straightforward design of Web Directions North[1]

Going to an event is meant to be an educational experience, especially when a workshop is involved. The Sidebar Workshops site we see in Figure 2.2 does this well by explicitly stating *What You'll Learn* right near the top of the page, and again right underneath the registration information. As

---

[1] http://north09.webdirections.org/

well as the prominent position, the text is short and easily digestible: a nice, memorable chunk to take away.

Figure 2.2. We know exactly what we'll gain from Sidebar Workshops[2]

Inventive and Innovative

Our client also wants us to ensure that the design suggests a feeling of invention and innovation. One way to present this idea with the most impact will be to create a design that breaks the rules slightly, whether that's in terms of color, layout, or type. As we look around for inspiration for our design, we'll be sure to keep our eyes out for examples that exemplify this goal. The real opportunity for trying something new will come later, however, when it's time to plan the aesthetics of the design—we'll get to that in Chapter 5.

Achieving a Balance: Information and Atmosphere

Balancing the display of information while conveying the right atmosphere is a huge challenge.

When I designed the Future of Web Applications (FOWA) Miami 2008 site,[3] I attempted to get the best of both worlds by giving the site a fun kind of feel with the beach in the background, but keeping the information neatly organized in the foreground. You can see this on the schedule page in Figure 2.3, with the clear separation of time slots and information. We decided that it would be more helpful if I designed some icons to visually indicate each type of session; that way, users could clearly see if it was a presentation, a lunch break, or a party, and so on. This allowed for the opportunity to throw a bit more of the playful feeling into the mix, so I threw in some *little dudes*.

---

[2] http://sidebarworkshops.com/2008/washingtondc/
[3] Unfortunately, this site is offline now.

14:05 — 14:45		**Panel Discussion, chaired by** Erick Schonfeld, **TechCrunch, including** Kevin Rose, **Digg** Launch a Web App in 40 Minutes
14:45 — 14:50		Sean Siebel, **Microsoft (Diamond Sponsor)**
14:50 — 15:30		Matt Marshall, **VentureBeat** What Makes The Next Great Startup?
15:30 — 16:10		Emily Boyd, **Remember The Milk** From the web, to the iPhone and beyond!
16:10 — 16:40		PM Break
16:40 — 17:20		Kevin Marks, **Google** The Future of APIs
17:20 — 18:00		Cal Henderson, **Flickr** The Application of New Features to an Established Application
18:00 — 18:40		Gary Vaynerchuk, **Winelibrary.tv** How to Grow a Community in The Future
19:00 — 20:00		**Live filming of Winelibrary.tv** Join Gary Vaynerchuk for a special filming of winelibrary.tv
21:00 — 01:00		**Official FOWA Party, sponsored by Scrapblog** @ Nikki Beach, South Beach, Miami

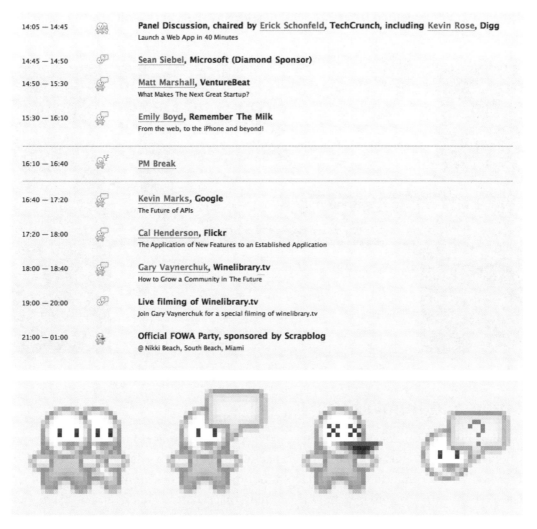

Figure 2.3. Adding fun to a schedule with some playful icons on the FOWA Miami 2008 site

The Sidebar guys kept the schedule looking fairly businesslike on their Workshops site, seen in Figure 2.4, but it still looks terrific, and is a great example of attention to detail.

TIME	DESCRIPTION	SPEAKER
8:00am – 9:00am	**Registration & Breakfast** Get to the hotel bright and early to pick up your namebadge and grab a snack before the first session.	
9:00am – 9:15am	Welcome & Introduction	
9:15am – 10:30am	**Planning & Designing Your Interface** You have a concept and a feature list, now what? Bryan helps you organize and label your content, and teaches you to find zen in the most subtle details.	Bryan Veloso
10:30am – 10:45am	**Mid-Morning Break** A quick pause between sessions—just enough time to grab some coffee and check your email.	
10:45am – 12:00pm	**Slicing & Dicing: Exporting & Optimizing Images** Now that you have your design, Dan teaches you to translate your carefully crafted layers into creatively flattened rectangles, and how to pick the best image type and compression to achieve the right balance of good looks and slim file sizes.	Dan Rubin
12:00pm – 1:15pm	**Lunch** Lunch will be catered in. This is a time to refuel, and get to know the other attendees and the speakers.	

Figure 2.4. More great design on the Sidebar Workshops site

What Matters the Most?

If you think about what might be the most important information relating to an event, you might say date, location, and price—but in all likelihood there are other elements that entice potential attendees.

Most events' web sites recognize celebrity appeal and make their big-name speakers as obvious as possible, like dConstruct,[4] shown in Figure 2.5. The reverse is also true: if the event lacks many web personalities, they'll play down the speaker list. Sometimes, as we see in Figure 2.6, the speaker list is so unwieldy that they choose to exclude it from the homepage altogether, and instead focus on more general information.

[4] http://2008.dconstruct.org/

Figure 2.5. Speakers are the priority on the 2008 dConstruct site's homepage ...

Figure 2.6. ... but the multitude of speakers at South by Southwest Interactive[5] means the homepage should house more general information

---

5 http://sxsw.com/

Venues and locations can sometimes be a drawcard for delegates. And when the location is also a popular holiday destination like Miami, then you should really shout about it.

Figure 2.7. The FOWA Miami 2009 site is unapologetic for its bold declaration of the location

Brand Consistency

Brand consistency is the goal of keeping a consistent look, feel, and message across all of a company's communications, including its web site. Depending on the project, you could find yourself in one of a number of potential situations. Let's take a look.

From Scratch

If the brand for the event is yet to exist, then our site will be providing the beginnings of a defined experience and acting as a style guide for other events to follow. Be mindful that limits may still apply, though: this might be the first event, but it should probably tie in with already established concepts by the company. That might translate to a simple action like incorporating the parent company's logo into the footer, or it may be more complex: there could be a particular set of style guidelines that we have to follow, such as a color scheme or font.

Redesign

If previous site designs exist, then you should maintain consistency, but each event could have its own *voice*, or theme. You can use previous versions of the site as a guide to design elements you could reuse. Perhaps you could use a different color palette, yet still maintain a similar design template.

Tie-ins

You may need to create a design that closely ties in with a previously established identity. The An Event Apart web site[6] seen in Figure 2.8 has its own branding, but incorporates the exact same look and feel of its sister site, A List Apart.[7] Rather than taking only small elements of the design patterns as you might find when a child site is borne of a parent company, the two are treated as equals: two sides to the same coin.

Figure 2.8. The literal tie-in of the web sites for An Event Apart and A List Apart

---

[6] http://aneventapart.com/
[7] http://alistapart.com/

For our project, we'll need to incorporate the company logo of the organization running the event—but we'll have free rein when it comes to the actual event branding, since it'll be the first of its kind (that is, the first scenario—From Scratch—above). This will demonstrate how you can be creative while still operating within a few guidelines. Guidelines are good, by the way: they take away some of the scare factor of a completely blank canvas!

Inspiration Resources

So far we've been looking to other events' web sites for inspiration, but we don't have to stick to that niche. It's become quite popular to collect examples of first-rate design and archive them as sets on Flickr,[8] an image-sharing service. To start off, check out Patrick Haney's massive collection,[9] and the Web Design Inspiration Flickr pool[10] which he administers. For even more Flickr sources, check out Vandelay Design's list of 99 Flickr groups for design inspiration.[11] And numerous web sites exist, such as Smashing Magazine[12] and UI Pattern Factory,[13] that are excellent sources of interesting design examples.

Atmosphere Inspiration

Let's get an idea of the kind of **atmosphere** we'd like our site to have—the feeling we evoke through color, subject matter, and texture. You may be familiar with the concept of a **mood board**, which describes a general collection of images, textures—almost anything that conveys the same *mood* you want to achieve. Let's take the term *wooden*: a traditional mood board might entail, for example, cutting out images of wooden furniture from catalogs or photographs of trees from magazines, and then laying them down on a canvas to make a montage.

Oh, and by the way, it's unnecessary to use an actual board—any surface (physical or virtual) will do! There is even a variety of software tools available to help you create your own mood boards if you want to do so digitally. Figure 2.9 shows a mood board created in Photoshop from public domain and Creative Commons-licensed images found on the Web.

---

[8] http://flickr.com/

[9] http://flickr.com/photos/splat/collections/72157600060481506/

[10] http://www.flickr.com/groups/webdesign-inspiration/

[11] http://vandelaydesign.com/blog/design/flickr-groups-for-designers/

[12] http://smashingmag.com/

[13] http://uipatternfactory.com/

Figure 2.9. A mood board[14]

Collating a photo set on Flickr is akin to the action of creating a mood board, particularly when researching atmosphere. I've collected some, which you'll see in Figure 2.10.

Figure 2.10. My atmosphere set on Flickr[15]

---

[14] This mood board incorporates images from the public domain and by Flickr members moriza, pshutterbug, extranoise, christophererin, caroslines and Ray_chel. They've been licensed under the Creative Commons Attribution license.
[15] http://www.flickr.com/photos/elliotjaystocks/sets/72157612161024243/

Composition Inspiration

We aim to create a unique and interesting web site, setting it apart from the kind of site you see every day. A noteworthy way to stand apart from the other sites is to think of an unusual composition or layout. We'll need to take a few risks in the interests of originality, so I've been collecting design examples which follow the same mantra. Of course, we'll still be mindful of the site's usability—it's important to stick with what users will understand—but you'll see that even a little *thinking outside the box* can go a long way. Here's my composition set on Flickr, in Figure 2.11.

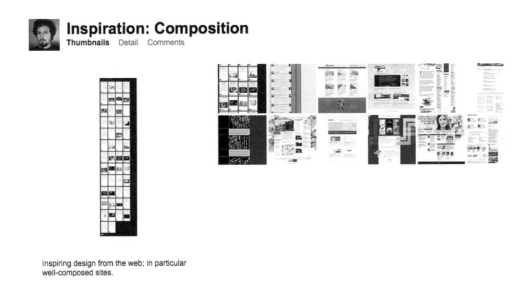

Figure 2.11. My set of composition examples[16]

Functionality Inspiration

Our site will contain a number of functional elements, like navigation mechanisms, a ticket purchase form, a schedule, and plenty more. It's useful to look at all the different ways other designers have chosen to implement each of these elements.

Chris Messina[17] has been collecting examples of user interface (UI) design on Flickr for years now, and his collections go beyond pure inspiration into the realm of an indispensable resource. You'll also find a wealth of UI examples collected at Pattern Tap,[18] where users have collected, tagged and commented on widgets from all over the Web.

---

[16] http://www.flickr.com/photos/elliotjaystocks/sets/72157612161071649/
[17] http://factoryjoe.com/
[18] http://patterntap.com/

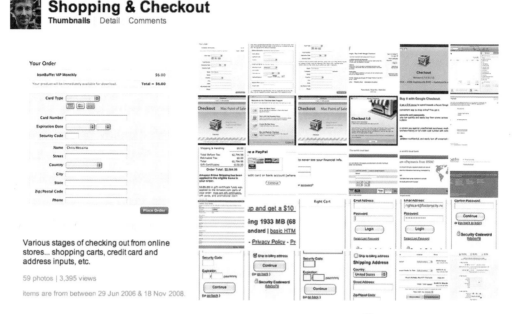

Figure 2.12. Chris Messina's design pattern sets on Flickr[19]

Look Outside the Web

I'm a keen believer in the idea that if you only use web sites for inspiration, you'll only ever build a web site that looks like other web sites. Of course there's nothing wrong with that—it's essential that a web site looks and behaves like one—but you risk your design growing stale if you search for stimuli in only one place.

There's a whole world out there full of outstanding design—architecture, fashion, product, packaging ... why confine yourself to one medium and limit your creative potential? Take your trusty camera and go for a walk—collect photos of signs, textures, anything that grabs your fancy. Doodle in a notebook whenever you have an interesting idea. Before you know it, you'll have a huge collection of inspiring material from the real world.

If you look at the world of print design in particular, you'll see most of the same principles of web design at work. After all, the new discipline of web design is derived from years of print design tradition, but with a few of the limitations and freedoms reversed. So there's still plenty of inspiration we can take from the print design world to better inform what we can achieve on the Web. I've collected some offline examples in—you guessed it—another Flickr set, shown in Figure 2.13.

---

[19] http://flickr.com/photos/factoryjoe/collections/72157600001823120/

Figure 2.13. My offline inspiration set

Collection Tools

I've been saving interesting and inspiring snippets in my Flickr profile, but it's not the only way.

RealMac Software[20]—the team behind web development application RapidWeaver—have recently released LittleSnapper,[21] a Mac application that allows you to collect sources of inspiration from the Web and share them with your peers. It's a nifty new tool for Mac-based designers, and one I'd heartily recommend.

For Windows users, TechSmith's Snagit[22] application captures screenshots and screen images, with a library you can use to organize your screenshots by tags, URLs, and date.

Then there's Evernote,[23] suitable for both Mac and Windows, an all-encompassing note-keeping application that you can access from just about everywhere, thanks to versions for your desktop, phone, and web browser. You can create, upload, and save images, text and audio, and if there's text contained within the image, Evernote's optical character recognition (OCR) engine will identify it and make it searchable. That's very handy for when your notes archive becomes rather large!

---

[20] http://realmacsoftware.com/

[21] http://realmacsoftware.com/littlesnapper/

[22] http://www.techsmith.com/screen-capture.asp

[23] http://www.evernote.com/

Figure 2.14. The extremely powerful Evernote

Figure 2.15. LittleSnapper, for happy snappers

Research: an Ongoing Process

Research is one of the most valuable ways to spend your time as a designer. Keep your eyes and mind open, and let yourself be influenced as much as possible. Ultimately, the more research you do, the more likely your design will be a success.

Chapter 3

Structure

It's time to think about the way we'll structure our design—so grab your paper and pen and get ready to doodle.

Let's make the most of our nice paper medium. First, let's make some loose sketches. And if you end up drawing characters and swirly lines instead of actual diagrams, that's fine too; if you feel like adorning the page with drawings that come from thoughts about events or events' web sites, feel free.

Remember what we were saying in Chapter 1: keep it loose.

 Notepads

Personally, I've always had a bit of a liking for small, blank pads wrapped in black hardcovers. I'm unsure what it is about them, but there's a quality I love about a blank page. Lineless ... margin-free ... just free rein to start creating. I'm a fan of the A5 size in particular (148mm × 210mm, or 5.8" × 8.3"—roughly the same size as a medium Moleskine notebook[1]) because it fits so neatly into your backpack; it's bigger than a reporter's notebook, but smaller than a professional artist's sketch pad.

---

[1] http://moleskine.com/

Figure 3.1. Some sketches for a recent project

Once you've warmed up your pen (and your brain!) it's time to start thinking about the way certain parts of our site will work. At this stage, it's unnecessary to worry about everything fitting neatly together; the idea is that we look at the overall picture before concentrating on precise details.

Sitemaps

You might have seen a **sitemap** on a web site—it's a list of many of the pages you'll find on that site. At the design stage, however, we'll use a sitemap as a way to draw our web site's structure like a map. But instead of thinking of them like a map that portrays the elements physically (like on an atlas), imagine them as a description of the way the pages link together. It's good to get a sitemap drawn before leaping into the design, because it gives you an understanding of how the site will work.

Initial Sketches

There are probably a number of ways to go about sketching a sitemap, but you might find it useful to write down the name of a page, draw a circle or rectangle around the word, and then use arrows to link it to other words. In Figure 3.2, you can see a loose, sketchy sitemap for Web in the Wild.

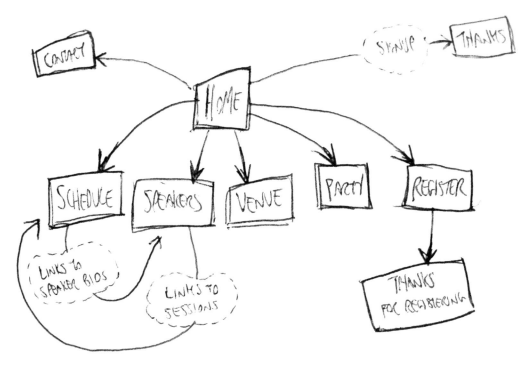

Figure 3.2. Getting some ideas down on paper

Web site pages rarely exist in isolation, and so there are often various ways (through different pages) to reach the same page. For instance, on our site's Schedule page, there'll be a listing of the sessions happening at the event which will include the speakers' names. Yet to access more information about each speaker, the names will be hyperlinked back to their profiles on the Speakers page. Likewise, there'll be links from those profiles back to the sessions. This demonstrates that there are more ways to reach the pages than by just using the main navigation bar.

Sitemaps versus Navigation

One thing I've struggled with in the past is the difference between writing down a navigation list and a sitemap. In essence, you might think that they're similar; after all, a navigation list is a list of pages on the site that the user can reach by clicking on the navigation items' names.

But what if you have a page like a legal notice that's pointless to display on your main navigation? Perhaps you might want to just keep it for a footer-based navigation bar? In that case, there's no way to tell that it's there unless you start with your sitemap first.

Another scenario is that you might have pages that are superfluous to any kind of navigation bar at all. This might sound strange at first, but imagine you have a sign-up form that allows users to receive your email newsletters. You'll probably want to have a *thanks* or *success* page that appears once they've successfully signed up; so that needs to be considered in the sitemap, even though it will never appear in a navigation bar or any kind of sitemap you show to users—this is just a sitemap for you, and for the people planning the project.

If you're planning out a process that happens without actually moving between pages (for instance, you might have a registration form that updates its contents using Ajax), it's worth creating separate diagrams to describe these processes, since it's potentially confusing to draw separate pages for this concept.

The important thing here is that it makes more sense to decide on your sitemap before your navigation, because you need to decide how the site fits together as a whole before deciding how it's navigated by your users.

Finished Diagrams

Once you've sketched through a few ideas and have settled on a sitemap concept you're happy with, it's a good idea to tidy it up. You could start by drawing a neater version (if, like me, your early sketches and notes are extremely rough!), or you could use some kind of visual editor to orderly display your ideas.

Applications like Microsoft Visio,[2] OmniGraffle,[3] or ConceptDraw MindMap[4] are popular tools to use, or you could simply use whatever tool you're comfortable with: there's nothing wrong with producing a sitemap in Photoshop or Illustrator.

I've recently started using WriteMaps,[5] a simple online tool for creating and sharing sitemaps. I like it because you can create a reasonably good-looking sitemap in seconds, like the one you see in Figure 3.3. Although it lacks the full functionality offered by desktop drawing tools, it more than makes up for it in ease of use. WriteMaps also provides you with a URL for each sitemap you make, which means it's extremely easy to share them with your clients or colleagues; plus you can export them to XML files if you need them later.

Personally, because I'm a picky, beard-stroking, beret-wearing designer (well, I was joking about the beret), I like to create the beginnings of a sitemap in WriteMaps, take a screen capture, and then neaten it up in Photoshop, ready to present the finished article to my client. You can see one of these in Figure 3.4.

---

[2] http://office.microsoft.com/en-us/visio/default.aspx
[3] http://omnigroup.com/applications/OmniGraffle/
[4] http://conceptdraw.com/en/products/mindmap/main.php
[5] http://writemaps.com/

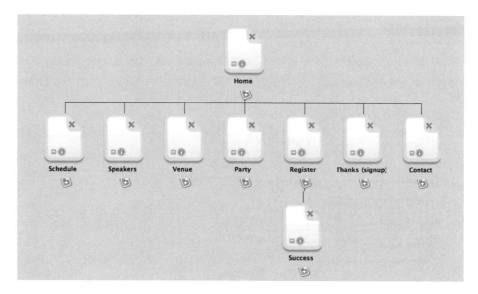

Figure 3.3. A sitemap created with WriteMaps

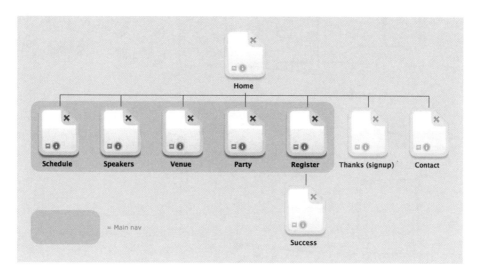

Figure 3.4. A finished sitemap

Some events sites have separate pages for sponsors, social networks, past events, and the like. For the sake of Web in the Wild, we'll keep it fairly simple and use only a small amount of pages.

Wireframing

Sitemaps deal with the structure of a web site; **wireframes** deal with the structure of individual pages. In a wireframe, we sketch out each page to try out different visual placements for each element.

Figure 3.5. One of my initial ideas for a layout

When creating a wireframe, what we're doing is thinking about how the elements work best on the page. We're considering which elements should be given prominence and how they best relate to each other.

Paper Prototyping

If you're more the hands-on type, you might like to try **paper prototyping**; a process where you print out (or draw) paper-based wireframes, cut out the elements, and move them about to see how they fit in different arrangements. And if you're working in a group, paper prototyping can be a great way to get instant, practical ideas from your team members—they'll be able to show you their suggestions right away, even if they're unable to draw a straight line with a ruler. We'll be sticking to notepads and sketches in this book, but if you'd like to give paper prototyping a try, there's a great introduction to the technique by Shawn Medero at A List Apart.[6]

Ways to Give Weight

There are various ways to make aspects of a web page prominent. Giving weight to an element can often be achieved using contrast (how it stands out from its surrounding elements), style (how it conforms to conventions, such as a certain look for links), and proximity (how it relates to nearby elements). Back in Figure 3.5, you can see how I've marked out a fat black box in the navigation panel to indicate a highlighted button marked "Buy"—this is where I'd like the Register button to go.

We'll be covering this in more detail in Chapter 5, but for now we'll focus simply on the placement of elements on the page. Of course, if you have any ideas right now about which elements ought to stand out, you should point these out in the sketch.

Our Checklist

Before we start sketching out some possible layout ideas, it'll help to list the elements that are going to appear on our pages.

Global Elements

Some of the most important elements should appear on every page. Let's make a quick list of these first:

- sponsor logo
- event title
- date
- venue
- navigation
- Register button

We can group all of these elements together in a *header* area. In fact, we can safely group the date and venue information into a kind of subheading within that header container.

---

[6] http://www.alistapart.com/articles/paperprototyping/

What else should appear on the site? Let's think about elements that should be on every page for now; that is, elements that will be in every template we design.

- secondary navigation
- contact details
- newsletter sign up

As far as we're concerned for our site, these are the only aspects that need to appear on all pages. We'll combine these into a *footer* area that will appear at the bottom, with the exception of the newsletter sign up: its position will vary from page to page. The reason for this is because we want it to appear on every page to increase the chance of people signing up, but we want to avoid it being shoved in their faces! Moving it around will help keep it looking fresh and prevent users feeling like they're experiencing a hard sell.

The Homepage

Like many sites—and in particular, events sites—our homepage will contain very little content. Instead, its focus will be on enticing users into the other areas of the site. It'll serve as an introduction to the rest of the site and offer bite-size chunks of tantalizing information to the visitor.

Underneath the header, we want to advertise these three important elements:

- featured speakers
- a brief introduction to the event
- a bit about the venue

The information below these three boxes is less important (well, depending on your viewpoint, perhaps), so it's safe to assume that it'll appear further down the page.

- information about the after party
- sponsor logos

The Schedule Page

- brief introduction
- table showing session schedule

The Speakers Page

- speaker bios and head shots

The Venue Page

- address
- travel info
- accommodation info
- photos of venue

The Party Page

- introduction
- party venue
- travel info
- sponsor details

The Registration and Tickets Page

- ticket types with price breakdown
- option to select ticket type
- contact details for assistance

When you have a clear idea of what needs to be on each page, it's time to start sketching them out for real.

Other Sites as Wireframe Sketches

If you're new to wireframing or find it hard to see its relevance, I'd encourage you to sketch rough layouts of your favorite web sites. It's about stripping off the *pretty* part of design and taking a look at the relation of elements on a page. For a real-world example, here are a couple of sketches I did of two existing events sites—FOWA Miami 2009, in Figure 3.6, and in Figure 3.7, Drupalcon DC 2009—alongside the finished results. You'll notice that even though the two sites have very different looks, the basic components—as well as their placement—are quite similar.

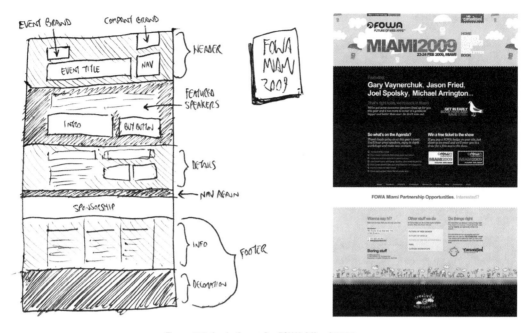

Figure 3.6. A wireframe for FOWA Miami 2009

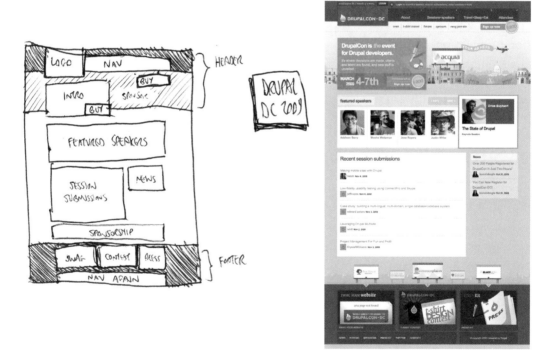

Figure 3.7. Drupalcon DC 2009

The Sketches

Label your sketches as you go, as it's surprisingly easy to forget what your various shaded boxes represent—especially if there'll be a lot of time between sketching out your first ideas and constructing a firmer wireframe.

Let's take a look at Figure 3.8, a sketch of our homepage in rough form.

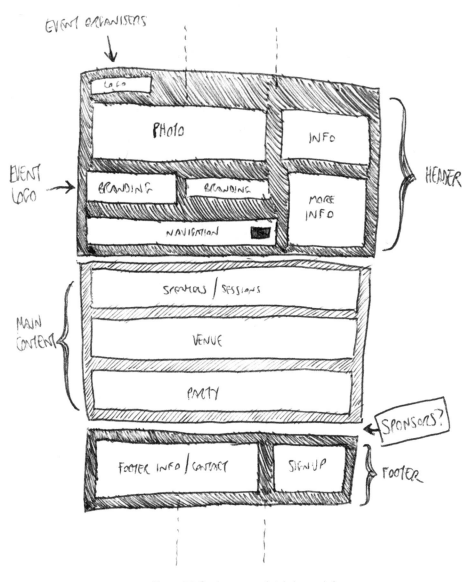

Figure 3.8. Our homepage sketch, in rough form

The Basic Template

Figure 3.9. A tidy wireframe

It's time to start tidying up a bit and creating a more solid wireframe: one that's more presentable to clients, clearer to work from, and closer to the final product. Since we need it to be neat and clear, it's finally okay to sit down with your computer! But take it easy: we'll still be sticking with plain representations of the layout at this point.

Instead of concerning ourselves with every element on the page, let's first focus on the core elements of the header and footer. We can use this as a basis for the wireframes for all our other pages. Figure 3.9 shows a tidier wireframe.

The Final Pages

With our basic template sorted, let's look at how the content area changes with each page. Dimensions and measurements are inexact right now: we'll finalize them when we start our layout in Photoshop.[7]

 Mix It Up a Bit

I really dislike web sites that retain the exact same look throughout all of the pages. Sure, consistency is extremely important, but sticking rigidly to a template without any room for customization outside of the main content area can quickly make things seem a little boring. We're all guilty of doing this to some degree, of course, but for this project I've chosen to add a little variety into the mix by varying the layout of the central elements between some of the pages. After all, even with a template system, we can still create a dynamic and interesting site.

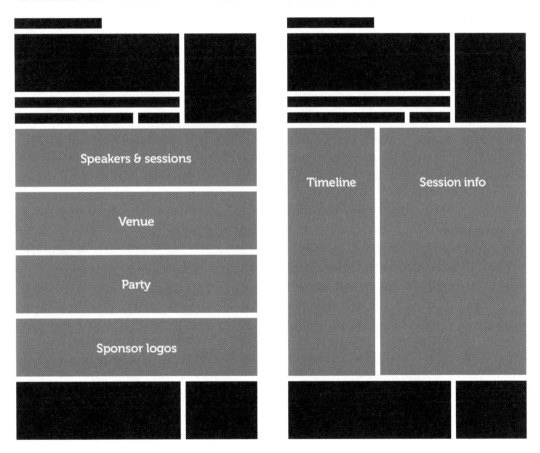

Figure 3.10. The homepage (left) and schedule (right)

---

[7] Due to printing constraints, the text is left out of the header and footer areas. The wireframes I'd give to my client would contain the text.

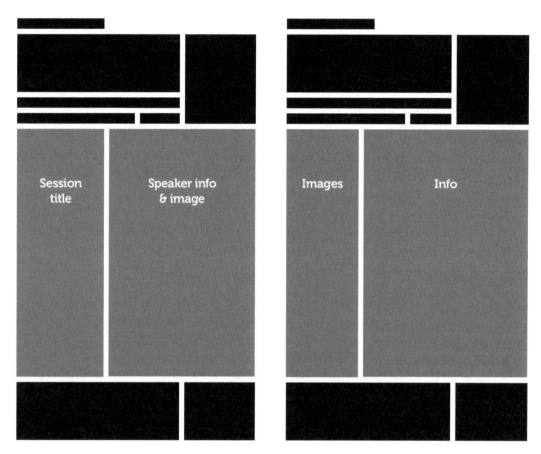

Figure 3.11. Speakers (left) and party (right)

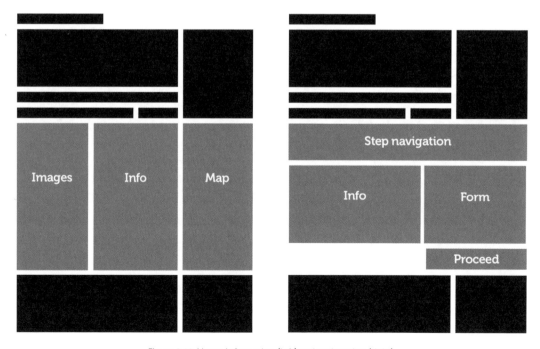

Figure 3.12. Venue information (left) and registration (right)

What Now?

We've constructed a kind of blueprint for the templates we'll build later in our project. Hopefully you're feeling much more confident about the creation of the design now that we've planned things out with these wireframes. Essentially, we've already made some of the toughest decisions. From here on in, it's going to be about turning the skeletal structures above into a living, breathing design.

Navigation and Interaction

As we've discussed previously in Chapter 1, there are various types of interactions that occur when a web site is visited. In this chapter, we'll be examining these and relating them back to our project. We'll need to address how our main navigation works, and what kind of enhancements we can build into the user interface to improve the browsing experience.

Because the core interactive experiences of the Web in the Wild site will be navigation and registering for the event, we'll be spending most of our time focusing on these.

Navigation

You've probably noticed when browsing the Web that a site's navigation appears near the top of the page; this ensures that you see the navigation when you first land on the site. But let's take a thorough look at this. Why is the navigation so important?

Consider this: a typical web site contains many pages, but without navigation they remain hidden on the server. If we were reading a conventional, paperbound book, we would eventually come across all the pages, regardless of whether there's a contents section—we'd discover what we wanted by flipping through it. This differs from the *wibbly wobbly* world of web design. Unless there are explicit links to the pages, users are unaware that they exist; perhaps the only way a user can access the hidden pages in this instance is by guessing the URLs. A navigation bar, like a table of contents in a book, gives us the ability to jump to various parts of the site, and also enables us to gain a sense of the site's breadth.

Of course, there's another way to find a page apart from using a navigation bar; the trusty search box, employed on many web sites (particularly large, multifaceted sites) is a helpful tool for finding any page or piece of information the user might require.

Figure 4.1. A combination of navigation bar and search on TasteBook[1]

Navigation = List

It's fair to say that navigation always takes the form of a list. But why use lists? Because they're a way of displaying important data in a simple, easy-to-read manner.

Let's take shopping, for example; imagine if we wrote out what we needed in prose form, as opposed to a list.

> "I'd like to buy some apples, and then I'll go down the next aisle and buy some tomatoes ... I think I'll buy some cherry tomatoes and perhaps some plum tomatoes too. After that I'll have a mooch around and see what else I need—maybe some chocolate biscuits and bread. Actually, I should probably grab a white loaf and a brown loaf. Oh, and some beer, of course!"

Imagine taking the time to write it out that way, trying to remember all that information, or glancing through that paragraph while doing your shopping! You can see why it's far more effective to write a list. And while doing so, we can group similar items together, since they're usually placed near each other and can be ticked off at the same time.

1. apples
2. tomatoes
   - cherry
   - plum
3. chocolate biscuits
4. bread
   - white
   - brown
5. beer

---

[1] http://tastebook.com/

Now we have a list that tells us the important information, grouping related information together in a useful way. That's a good analogy for the way we'd like to organize our navigation.

Sometimes It's Okay to Bend the Rules

Even though we've just seen how important information benefits from being displayed in a simple list, there are exceptions. On the Happy Cog site, shown in Figure 4.2, you can see how prose is used to wrap up the navigation terminology. The sentence is short so it's easily digestible, and it adds a nice little spin on the traditional method of navigation.

Figure 4.2. Happy Cog's unorthodox but clear navigation panel

Navigation in the Online World

We create lists in much the same way when we plan the structure of a web site's navigation system. Bigger topics can be the top level of the menu, and subtopics can act as submenus. The submenus might appear as drop-downs when we hover over an item, or they might appear on a separate page if there are a lot of them. In fact, there are many types of navigation, but what we need to consider is the hierarchy of the information and how that's presented, as well as the grouping of related or similar elements.

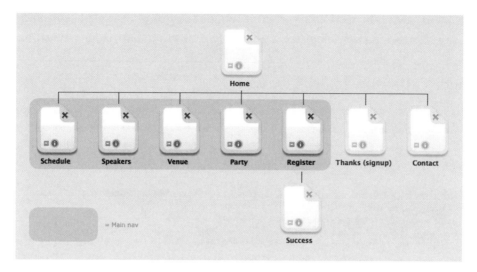

Figure 4.3. Our sitemap, again

Let's jump back to the sitemap we created in the previous chapter, shown in Figure 4.3. Here's a list of the pages we're going to have on our event site:

1. Home
2. Schedule
3. Speakers
4. Venue
5. Party
6. Register
7. Newsletter signup (thanks)

As we've discussed previously, the newsletter sign-up page will be excluded from the navigation panel—since we'll be placing a sign-up box in every page of the site, most likely in the sidebar, it doesn't need to be shown as a separate page.

The Problematic Homepage Button

Another question we should ask before pushing ahead is: should we explicitly link back to the homepage with a *Home* button, or should the logo simply act as a homepage link?

Opinions in the web community differ on this argument. As a general rule, I think that the homepage is worth specifically linking back to in the navigation bar if its content is significantly different from that of the other pages. For example, the homepage of a newspaper site might also have extra features found only on that particular page within the site, such as a weather widget or videos. Otherwise, it's safe to leave off.

However, it's often a good idea to link the web site's logo or title to the homepage, as this is a common convention that many users now expect. It's worth doing it whether you have a separate Home button or not.

Web in the Wild, like the vast majority of web sites, will have a variety of content on its homepage; specifically, snippets of content from around the site. In this sense, it deserves a Home button in the main navigation. There. Sorted. Lovely!

Navigation Types

So far, we've been talking about the main or global navigation; that is, navigation that appears on every page of the site, allowing us to reach each main page. Our web site is a simple one with only a few pages, but it's still useful to think about some different types of navigation and how they could fit into our site. We'll use some inspiration from around the Web to see some of the ways each kind of navigation can be used.

Global Navigation

As we discussed above, the global navigation is the menu that appears on every page of the site and links to all of the main pages. The examples from Figure 4.4 and Figure 4.5 show navigation arranged as horizontal strips, while those in Figure 4.6 and Figure 4.7 arrange the items vertically.

Figure 4.4. Horizontal navigation on 13 Creative[2]

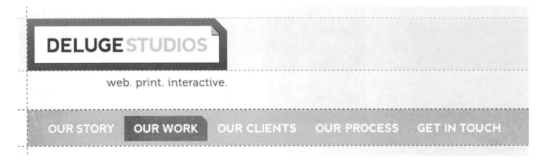

Figure 4.5. ... and on Deluge Studios[3]

---

[2] http://13creative.com/
[3] http://delugestudios.com/

Figure 4.6. Vertical navigation on the Emblematiq[4] portfolio site

Figure 4.7. ... and another example on Cameråon.io[5]

Supporting Navigation

Supporting navigation is used to supplement global navigation. Usually, it contains links to pages that you'd like to have on every page, but don't need to have the same visual weight as your global navigation—like a privacy policy page, a help link, or an account login button.

---

[4] http://emblematiq.com/
[5] http://cameron.io/

Figure 4.8 and Figure 4.9 show two different ways to treat these links: the first, from Movable Type,[6] places supporting navigation near the global navigation; the second, from SitePoint[7], shows a small bar that sits at the bottom of every page.

Figure 4.8. Movable Type's supporting navigation, sitting above the main one ...

Figure 4.9. ... and SitePoint's at the bottom

Local Navigation

Local navigation, like the kind shown in Figure 4.10, guides a user to certain sections in a long page. These could be handy on our Schedule page, if a user wants to jump to a particular session.

Figure 4.10. Clicking a speaker's name (top) on the Web Directions North speakers page[8] scrolls the page down to the bio (bottom)

---

[6] http://movabletype.com/

[7] http://sitepoint.com/

[8] http://north.webdirections.org/speakers/

Breadcrumb Trails

Breadcrumb trails, just like the breadcrumbs from the Hansel and Gretel story, are employed to show a user a path. On the Web this usually means a path from the homepage to the page they're looking at, or a series of steps within a process. For example, the breadcrumb trail from the Apple Store UK,[9] shown in Figure 4.11, displays a series of three steps that match the actions I've taken—I've been to the shop, I've chosen a MacBook Pro, and now I'm at the configuration screen.

Figure 4.11. Breadcrumbs on the Apple Store UK

We'll use similar breadcrumbs in our design to guide users through the ticket-ordering process.

Search

A search bar, like the one in Figure 4.12, provides a quick and easy place for a user to start searching your site. Traditionally, when a user enters a search term and submits the form, they would then see a page displaying those search results.

It's recently become more feasible to present search results right away, as soon as the user finishes typing, as seen in Media Temple's knowledge base.[10] As we can see in Figure 4.13, the results appear in a floating box that sits right underneath the search field you were typing in, rather than using an entirely new page.

Figure 4.12. Get Satisfaction's search bar[11]

[9] http://store.apple.com/uk/
[10] http://kb.mediatemple.net/
[11] http://getsatisfaction.com/

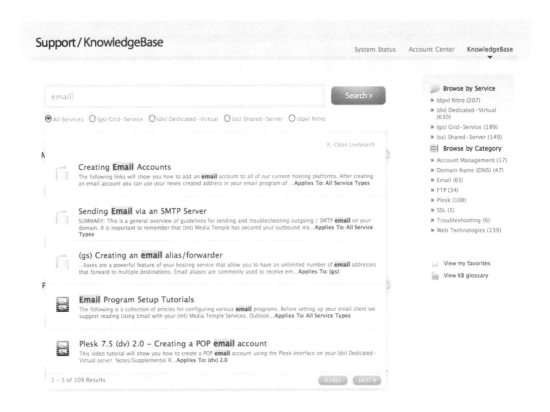

Figure 4.13. Media Temple's live search

Pagination

Pagination provides a way to divide up a large chunk of information, like a large set of blog posts or a long magazine article, into more manageable pages. It's quite common on larger sites, where there's a lot of information to be explored. Since our site is quite small, pagination will be unnecessary, but it's worth knowing about as a form of navigation anyway.

Pagination usually includes a set of pages, a clear indicator of which page you're on, and a way to move backwards and forward between the pages. In Figure 4.14, we can see a fairly typical example of pagination as seen on design blog Design Reviver.[12]

Figure 4.14. Pagination in action

Navigation Styles

Of course, there are many ways to style our navigation. We tend to think of global navigation elements as *bars* or *menus*, but sub-navigation elements can be very different, as we've seen.

---

[12] http://designreviver.com/

Each *style* of navigation carries with it certain expectations: in other words, if the navigation takes the form of tabs, you'll be expecting it to behave like tabs.

Lists

We've already talked about navigation elements as being lists; if you're comfortable with HTML, you probably already know that the best way to mark up a navigation element is as a list. However, from a graphical point of view, we probably perceive navigation lists as a simple collection of words, expressed top-to-bottom or left-to-right.

In terms of style, we have a lot of room for flexibility. Global navigation will be bold and obvious, and often blocky. Sub-navigation, like a category listing, would more likely be rendered smaller or plainer to indicate that it's further down in the hierarchy. We can see the contrast in an example of this kind in Jesús Rodríguez Velasco's site,[13] shown in Figure 4.15, between the bold main navigation and the more subtle list of dates that make up the sub-navigation menu.

Drop-down Menus

A form of navigation almost as old as web design itself, **drop-down menus** provide a handy way of showing a submenu without cluttering up the page. That's because they only appear when a user wants them to, by clicking on or hovering over the link.

Drop-downs come in two flavors: the more traditional ones resemble the kind of menu you'd find in web forms. A popular way to use these is as a country or language chooser, as shown on the Apple site[14] in Figure 4.16.

Figure 4.15. Contrast in Jesús Rodríguez Velasco's navigation styles

---

[13] http://jrvelasco.com/
[14] http://www.apple.com/

Figure 4.16. Choose your country at Apple

The other kind of drop-down is typically triggered when a user rolls over a menu item—you'll sometimes hear these called **rollover menus**. In the past these were commonly made by using JavaScript, although as browser support for CSS has improved, these menus are often made with CSS. Figure 4.17 shows us a fairly complex example from Media Temple, while the menu on Designsensory[15], shown in Figure 4.18 is quite a lot simpler.

Figure 4.17. A drop-down menu at Media Temple

Figure 4.18. A simpler menu on Designsensory's site

---

[15] http://www.designsensory.com/profile/

Tabs

Tabs suggest that the content they link to is all part of the same cohesive whole. The tab metaphor is borrowed from a real-world desk—or, more specifically, the tabbed hanging folders you might find in your desk drawers. Just as we can quickly and easily flip between tabs in a folder or in our operating system, it's common to see the content of tabs appear without a page reload. Sometimes the transition between content areas is animated in some way, for example, swishing from left/right or right/left. This technique became extremely popular again after Panic, a software company, utilized the effect on their site, seen in Figure 4.19. Obviously it's difficult to demonstrate animation in a printed book, so I definitely recommend you visit the Coda site[16] to see it in action.

Figure 4.19. The CSS tab is selected on Panic's Coda web site

---

[16] http://panic.com/coda/

Collapsible/Expandable

I mentioned how tabs mimic desktop behavior, but so do other navigation styles. Dragging and dropping is another desktop metaphor, like picking up and moving pieces of paper, and—of particular interest in terms of navigation—expanding and collapsing.

The recent popularity (in the last couple of years) of flexible, easy-to-implement JavaScript libraries have ensured that adding animated effects to a site is now commonplace on the Web; limitations to the realms of Flash or extremely complex JavaScript are now a past concern. One interface effect that's become particularly popular is the collapsible/expandable menu. This is sometimes referred to as an **accordion menu**—the effect resembles the way an accordion file folder expands and contracts while you flip through it.

Some examples house actual content, as shown on the moo.fx[17] site seen in Figure 4.20—each item expands to show a paragraph of text—while others use the technique to show and hide sub-menu items as a replacement for the traditional drop-downs.

Figure 4.20. Collapsible/expandable content on Moo.fx

---

[17] http://moofx.mad4milk.net/

Tag Clouds

A visually interesting way to present a set of topics is in the form of a **tag cloud**—a series of words that use size and prominence to indicate a particular term's popularity or importance, so named for the way the group of terms resemble the puffy outline of a cloud.

Tag clouds are a particularly interesting form of navigation, because they imply a sense of what topics are most discussed by allowing some tags to appear in larger or smaller font sizes. As a general rule, the larger the font size, the more popular the tag. For example, in the tag cloud on Web Designer Wall[18]—seen in Figure 4.21—it's fairly clear at a glance that that the Inspiration topic is quite a lot more well-covered than SEO, search engine optimization.

The knock-on effect is that the links within tag clouds are usually dynamic in two different ways: firstly, their size is constantly subject to fluctuation as the content on the site changes, and secondly, the terms that form the tag cloud are also updated as soon as new topics are introduced. Some sites—where many tags are supported—will only display the most popular; this results in a form of navigation that regulates itself with little effort required from the person(s) behind the web site.

Figure 4.21. A tag cloud on Web Designer Wall

---

[18] http://webdesignerwall.com/

Tool Tips

Another technique that's become popular with the increased use of lightweight JavaScript libraries is the adding of bubbles that resemble tool-tips when the user hovers over an item that requires additional explanation. This is less a form of navigation and more an augmentation, but it's still useful to add to our tool kit.

An excellent example of this technique can be found on Panic's site, with information displayed about the product above the *Download* link, shown in Figure 4.22.

Figure 4.22. Handy information in a tooltip on the Coda site

Our Use of Navigation

Although we'll decide on the visual look of our navigation when we deal with aesthetics—which we'll do in the next chapter—we can still define the various types and styles we'll plan to use right now:

- global navigation—a left-to-right list
- local navigation—jump menus for the schedule page
- breadcrumb trails—used to indicate progress in the ticket-ordering service
- search bar—at the top of each page with a Results page template to display the result

Forms

When creating forms, the aim is to achieve a balance between gaining as much information from your site visitor as possible without making them feel as though they have to fill in too many fields. Asking for too much information will simply turn people away, so the key is to be as succinct as you can.

If you need to display supplementary information, you could do it using small pieces of text that appear when certain form elements are selected, or use notes to inform users of an error in their form entries. In Figure 4.23, the sign-up form for Ning,[19] we can see an example of errors being indicated with highlighting on the form fields, along with a note at the top.

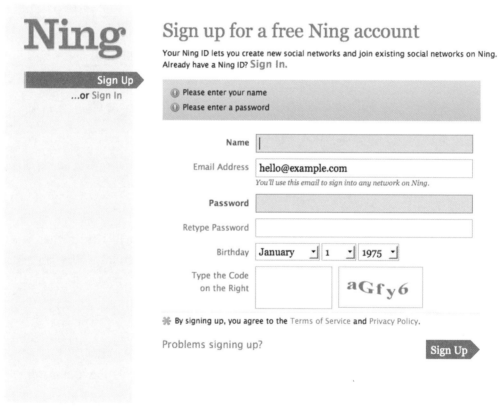

Figure 4.23. A form error from Ning

Web forms often ask the user to read additional information before completing the form—for example, a competition entry form would have terms and conditions attached, or a form that collects personal information would need to refer to the web site's privacy policy. If your project requires it, you'll need to think about how those work and where you'd like to place them. Looking back at Figure 4.23,

[19] http://ning.com/

we can see the Ning developers have chosen to place these links at the bottom and highlight the line with a small icon.

Form design and usability is a fairly complex topic that deserves more time than we can give it in this book. For a comprehensive read on form interaction, I'd suggest you take a look at *Web Form Design: Filling In The Blanks,*[20] by Luke Wroblewski—it's based on solid research into successful form design, and filled with examples of usable *and* sexy forms.

Our Use of Forms

As you know, we're building an uncomplicated web application, so our use of forms on the event's web site is going to be relatively sparse. We'll be using forms for:

- search functionality
- newsletter sign-up
- ticket-buying process

Audio-visual Content

Let's imagine that the organizers of Web in the Wild have commissioned a video designed to entice people along. We'll want to include that video on the homepage.

Complex versus Minimal

Online video is extremely common these days, with most videos being displayed using the Flash video (FLV) format. While some of these sites use complex, feature-packed video players, others go for a minimal approach, keeping controls mostly out of the way. This is potentially a good move to take if you only intend to use video as a simple showcase, secondary to the content on the rest of the site.

To showcase some of the features of their music production software Live, Ableton employ a video player that's minimalist in the extreme. When the user's cursor moves away from the player, the control/progress bar vanishes. This is tricky to show on paper, so I'll recommend you head over to their site[21] to see it disappear for yourself.

---

[20] http://www.lukew.com/resources/web_form_design.asp
[21] http://ableton.com/live/

Figure 4.24. Ableton Live's minimal video

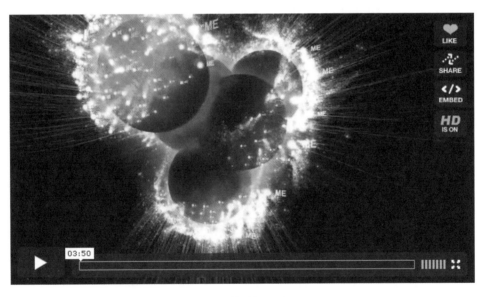

Figure 4.25. The Vimeo player

The same technique is used by Vimeo,[22] shown in Figure 4.25. The video player's interface—when shown—exhibits the *Share* buttons associated with video-sharing sites, but does so in a minimal and visually pleasing way. Sites like Vimeo have recognized that the video should be allowed to *breathe* without users worrying about how to control it.

---

[22] http://vimeo.com/

By comparison, the YouTube player shown in Figure 4.26 is more complex—there are several buttons, which remain on the screen for the duration of the movie, and a menu full of options at the bottom right.

Figure 4.26. YouTube's player: somewhat less subtle

Our Use of Video

We'll need to design a minimal video player with some very simple controls:

- play/pause
- volume
- loading/progress bar; usually you can grab this to jump back and forth in the movie (this is often called a **scrub bar**)

Because we want our video to be unobtrusive, we should have sound off by default. This presents a problem, though: we'll need to make sure that site visitors know sound can be turned on. Therefore, we'll need to add a couple more controls:

- auto-replay on/off
- sound on/off

Ecommerce

If you're looking for a book on the subject of ecommerce design, I'd heartily recommend *WEB Design: E-Commerce*[23](Köln: Taschen, 2007). As the breadth of ecommerce design is too wide to cover in detail here, I'm simply going to deal specifically with how we'll be using ecommerce in the ticket-buying process of the site.

Our Use of Ecommerce

In the main navigation bar, there'll be an item called Register; this will be given much more prominence than any of the other items, since enticing visitors to book tickets is the primary goal of the site (as defined in Chapter 2).

Clicking this button will take the user to a Bookings page, and within that page, there'll be a five-step process. Let's explain it in this simple flow diagram:

Step 1: Site displays an introductory panel page → Step 2: User enters contact info → Step 3: User selects ticket types → Step 4: User enters payment details → Step 5: Site shows a confirmation message.

In other words, the bookings section comprises five pages, with each page representing a stage in the booking process.

At this point, it's a good idea to sketch it out so we're clear on how this will work. You can see my sketch in Figure 4.27.

Figure 4.27. A sketch of the bookings process

[23] http://www.amazon.com/gp/product/3822840556/

While it might seem strange to point out every step in such detail, there's an important lesson to be learned here: examining the details of interaction and, where necessary, creating interaction diagrams, are a vital part of establishing how your site should be used. Creating design wireframes (like we did in the previous chapter) will only tell you so much about interaction. You have to then look into the details of interaction and build upon the outline you established in your wireframes.

Finalizing Interaction

We're now ready to start designing the various elements we've talked about in this chapter. How exciting! But hang on a moment…

A Slight Change of Plan

It's a fact of life that in the process of designing a web site, your client is going to want to make some adjustments, and that time has come for our project. Let's imagine that a request has just come in from our client.

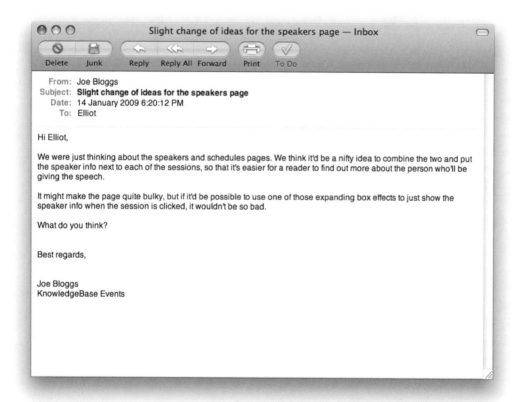

What do I think? I think that sounds pretty good. We could quite easily include the speakers' information (a short biography, headshot, and URL) in a box near each of the sessions. They could be collapsed by default and only open when clicked on by the user. And to keep it tidy, opening one speaker info panel should automatically close any other that is currently open. Let's sketch out some ideas and see how it looks: you'll see mine in Figure 4.28.

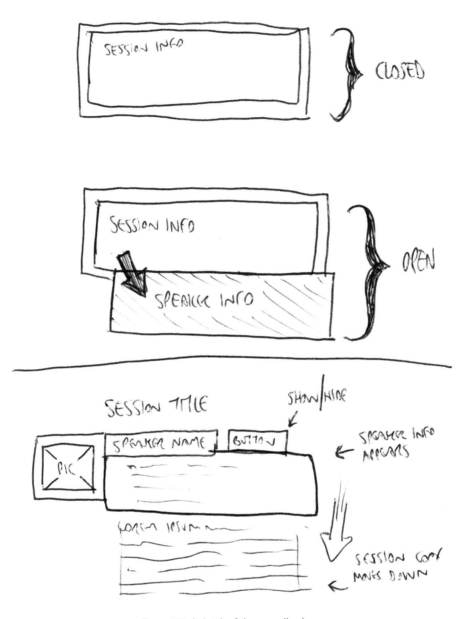

Figure 4.28. A sketch of the expanding boxes

Lovely!

Conclusion

There are many forms of interaction that happen on a web site, from clicking on navigation items to finding your way around content, through to drilling down into directories and interacting with forms, and everything in between.

In order to keep the user on our site, we need to engage them. We can do this by offering a positive experience: one that allows them to find information quickly and easily, and prevents any obstacles from being in their way. This can be achieved by following the usability and accessibility guidelines we've discussed in previous chapters, as well as following tried and tested web design conventions that give the user the experience they're expecting. Using comfortable conventions from the desktop and the offline world, our aim is to make it as easy for the user as possible: a relaxed web site visitor is a happy one.

But in order to fully capture a user's attention and make the web site as easy to use as possible, we're going to make it look great. No, better than great: *sexy*! In the next chapter, we'll be taking on our biggest task yet: the challenge of aesthetics.

Chapter **5**

Aesthetics

As I said in Chapter 1, aesthetics are what I consider to be the fun part of design. It's the part of the process that deals exclusively with making our project sexy!

It can be very easy, with deadlines looming and technical difficulties prevailing, to cut corners with aesthetics. But it's so important to do it properly, because that extra layer of care goes such a long way. The difference between good design and great design can often be subtle, but subtlety works on a subconscious level: people will be impressed by good design without knowing it, but great design will thrill them. They'll love what they see, and they'll come back for more. And with the whimsical, temporary, intangible nature of web design, it's so important to motivate your visitors to return.

Before we start, here's a quick word about the build stage: as you know, we're dealing only with design rather than code in this book, but it's still important that you consider how all of these design elements might be executed once it's time to develop the site—in case you create a design that's unnecessarily difficult to build. We'll be exploring this idea further in Chapter 6, but we'll also be keeping this in mind as we think of aesthetics.

A Small Introduction to Layout and Composition

Rather than go into detail about layout and composition theory, I will first refer you to *The Principles of Beautiful Web Design,*[1] written by Jason Beaird (Melbourne: SitePoint, 2007). The book's first

---

[1] http://www.sitepoint.com/books/design1/

chapter is all about composition, and it's available for free at SitePoint.[2] If you're new to the web game, or even design generally, I'd recommend it as a good starting point.

Should you be concerned I'm going to send you off to Jason's book and put my feet up? Well, actually, there's still a lot we need to discuss! We'd started to tackle layout and composition already when we created our wireframes in Chapter 3. They were only very rough, though, helping us to work out element placement in a very loose sense. Now we'll be looking at page layout in a more precise manner.

Art and Design Traditions

There's a good reason that many of the principles used in art and print design have carried across to the Web. We've mentioned before that our primary focus is on making sexy web sites, and that's certainly most true when we're talking very specifically about aesthetics. So it makes perfect sense, then, to consider these traditional techniques.

The Golden Ratio

The golden ratio (sometimes called the *divine proportion*) is a magical-sounding phrase used to describe an aesthetically pleasing way to divide an area into two parts, arrange objects within an frame, or create a well-proportioned rectangle. It's fascinated everyone from Greek mathematicians to Renaissance painters to today's graphic designers, and now it's time to add it to your toolbox, too. Rest assured—I'll steer clear of bogging you down with mathematics, but essentially the magic number is approximately *1.62*. Divide any length by that and you'll find the point where you can draw a dividing line. This is 61.2% of the total length—a little under two thirds. In Figure 5.1, you'll see a rectangle using the golden ratio—its height is 61.2% of its length, and it's divided in two parts according to this principle as well.

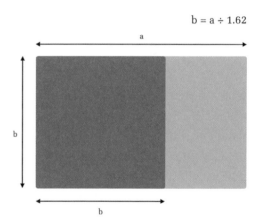

Figure 5.1. The golden ratio, demonstrated

If you're one of those people who always tries to avoid dealing with numbers, you can use the Golden Ratio Calculator[3] instead. It takes a number, and gives you instant answers and nifty visual feedback. In Figure 5.2, you can see how a figure I've entered (960 pixels) is shown as a part of some different ratio-based layouts.

---

[2] http://www.sitepoint.com/article/principles-beautiful-web-design/
[3] http://goldenratiocalculator.com/

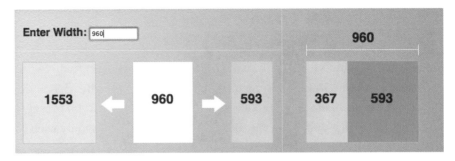

Figure 5.2. The Golden Ratio Calculator does all the heavy lifting

The Rule of Thirds

A simpler version of the same principle is the **rule of thirds**. One way to use this is to divide your designs into thirds, fill two thirds with content, and leave one third for whitespace. Another way might be to use the rule of thirds to help determine the width or placement of a sidebar within your design.

You can see this in action in Figure 5.3, which shows a variety of layout ideas using this principle.

Figure 5.3. The rule of thirds

Fixed or Flexible?

Because of the flexible nature of web sites, and the variable size of users' browser windows, we only have a limited area in which to work. Mostly this is down to the fact that we have to cater for the average user; that is, those with small screens. As such, it would be unwise to design a site wider than 1,000 pixels, since users on a 1,024 × 768px resolution would be presented with horizontal scrollbars. As of December 2008, 1,024 × 768px remained the most widely used resolution—up to 48% of users.[4]

More importantly, we have less than 1,000 pixels to work with generally, as some of that window is occupied by toolbars, tabs, or other parts of the browser's interface, called **browser chrome**. The remaining viewable space in the browser window is the space where your site will be displayed—this is called a **viewport**.

This can be a challenge, because we're unable to predict whether a user will visit with the browser window maximized, or how much browser chrome is occupying some of the space inside the window. Many users' windows appear at a variety of widths—especially on a Mac, where maximizing behaves differently than in Windows; even on large screens, whether a user will have a window open at anywhere near its maximum width and height is indeterminable. What's more, we're unaware of how large the user's text will be; since it's possible to set a preferred font size in the browser's preferences, those choices could affect the way text is displayed in our design.

Fortunately, we have some options available that will help us take advantage of this flexibility.

---

[4] We've used statistics from W3 Schools (http://www.w3schools.com/browsers/browsers_display.asp) and TheCounter.com (http://www.thecounter.com/stats/2008/December/res.php).

Fixed, Fluid, or Elastic Layouts

Web layouts can be described as fixed, fluid (or sometimes liquid), or elastic.

With a **fixed** layout, the dimensions of the layout are specified in a particular number of units—usually pixels. In Figure 5.4, we can see a basic example of a fixed width layout, 750 pixels wide; whether it's shown in a smaller or larger window, you can see that the layout remains the same size.

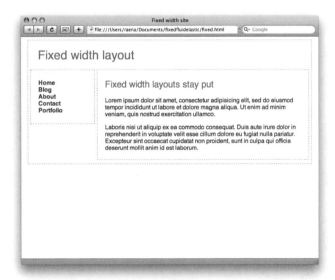

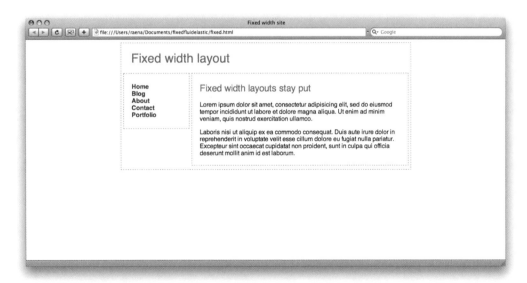

Figure 5.4. A fixed layout stays the same size in larger and smaller windows

A **fluid** or **liquid** layout's dimensions are defined relative to the size of the viewport using percentages. Figure 5.5 shows a fluid layout specified at 60% width in two differently sized windows. One of the challenging aspects in this particular example is that the text occupies more vertical space when the window is narrow.

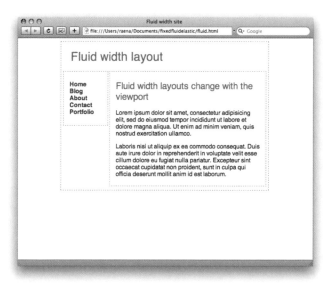

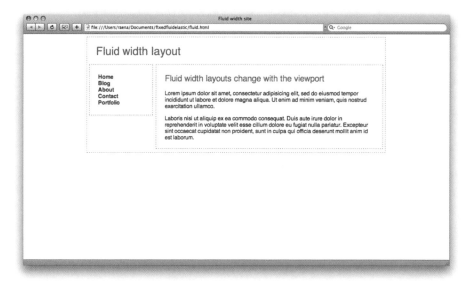

Figure 5.5. This fluid layout occupies 60% of the width, regardless of the size of the window

An **elastic** layout's dimensions are dependent on text size. In Figure 5.6, the layout's width has been specified at **60 em units**.[5] The first window shows the text at the default browser size, and the second shows what happens if the browser's text size is increased; you can see how the entire layout has expanded proportionally to the text size.

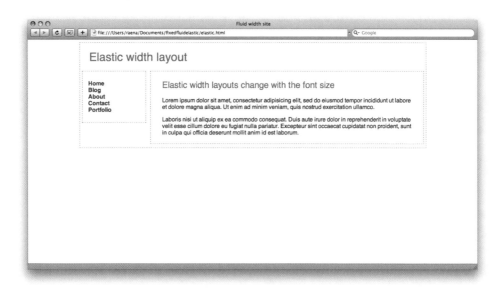

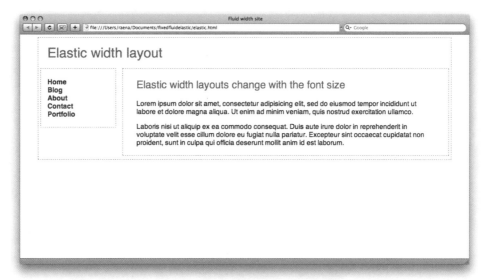

Figure 5.6. This elastic layout expands with the text.

---

[5] In his book, *The Elements of Typographic Style* (Hartley and Marks: Vancouver, 1992), Robert Bringhurst says that "[t]he em is a sliding measure. One em is a distance equal to the type size. In six point type, an em is six points; in 12 point type an em is 12 points, and in 60 point type an em is 60 points. Thus a one em space is proportionately the same in any size."

You can read more about the pros and cons of each option all over the Web, as it's a topic that's been hotly debated for some time, but I'll start you off with two good summaries: *CSS Layouts: The Fixed. The Fluid. The Elastic.*[6] by Mike Cherim, and *Fixed, Fluid, or Elastic Width Layouts?*[7] by Anup Shah.

As you might imagine, it can be difficult to represent the nuances of an elastic or fluid design in a static Photoshop comp. It would be unrealistic for us to show every possible width, but presenting two variations to your client would help them understand the idea, especially if they're unfamiliar with the difference between fixed and variable layouts.

In the design for Web in the Wild, we'll be sticking with a fixed-width design to make the most of the precise measurements for which pixels allow.

Horizontal Scrolling

Another way to create a contrasting look is to scroll the content sideways. Because it's a bit out of the ordinary to have a site that scrolls horizontally, you can see some designers experimenting with this effect. On Tyler Finck's site, Sursly,[8] he uses the shape of his background images to make it appear as if areas of color are growing or shrinking as you click between each of the GO arrows. These arrows help indicate how the interface moves between each part of the content, as you can see in Figure 5.7, which helps avoid any possible confusion by users unfamiliar with this method of navigation.

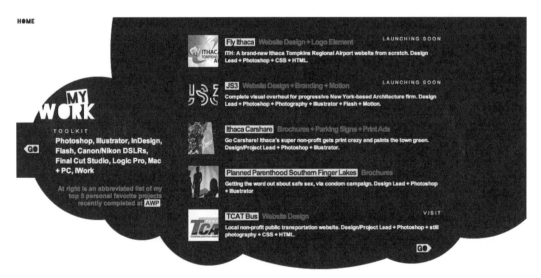

Figure 5.7. A portion of Sursly

[6] http://green-beast.com/blog/?p=199

[7] http://onenaught.com/posts/9/fixed-fluid-or-elastic-width-layouts/

[8] http://sursly.com/

The Grid

In design, a grid works around the premise that visual information is easier to digest if elements are in alignment—horizontally or vertically. The average viewer will probably be unaware, consciously, of the alignment, but like with so many aesthetic principles, the satisfaction they experience happens on an almost subliminal level. And if the eye moves around the page naturally, we're talking major brownie points for usability!

Like most web design principles, the grid is inherited from the world of print. And that, too, is taken from the world of art. Grid systems have been present in art and architecture for millennia, from the ancient Egyptian representation of human proportion, the ancient Greeks' Parthenon, and European Renaissance art (incorporating the golden ratio discussed earlier).

Using Grids

With a decent grid setup, it's relatively easy to align elements and decide on their sizes. It's helpful to set up a grid with Photoshop's **Guides** feature, as shown in Figure 5.8:

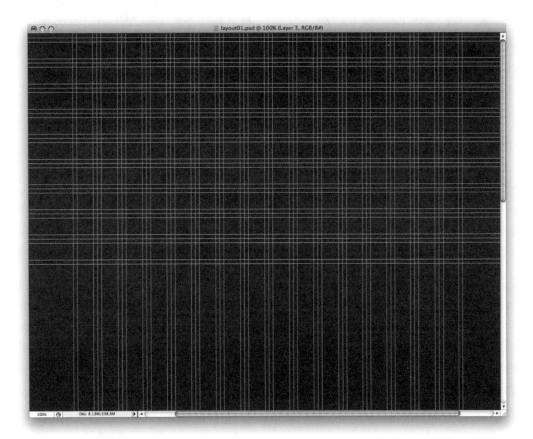

Figure 5.8. This document has lots of guides

I'm a big fan of the 960 Grid System,[9] which is a free downloadable framework from Nathan Smith. You can use its CSS and markup as a base for building sites, although I prefer to just use its Photoshop templates, since I have my own web development framework.

The 960 Grid System contains two Photoshop files: one that's divided into 12 columns and one that's divided into 16. The 960 figure is used because it is divisible by so many different numbers, making it a perfect measurement for designing sites within the 1000-pixel boundary we discussed earlier. This saves you having to think about all those measurements yourself! In Figure 5.9, you can see the basic page layout from the wireframes we created back in Chapter 3. To its right is the same layout, but with the 960 Grid System columns overlaid for clarity.

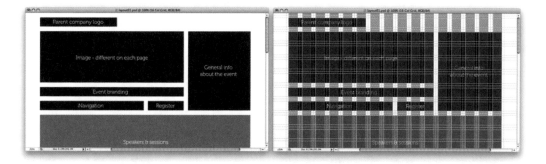

Figure 5.9. Our wireframes, hiding (left) and revealing the grid (right)

Other frameworks you might like to try out include the Yahoo User Interface Library's Grid[10] and Blueprint.[11] Both are especially useful if you're new to markup and want to use a system that has much of the code in place. It also takes some of the tedious arithmetic out of the equation!

Breaking Out of the Grid

Of course, great design is about being aware of the rules and also knowing when to break them. Sticking rigidly to a grid system can sometimes lead to a restricted, predictable design. Innovation is about trying a different approach, and ground-breaking designs are the kind we're interested in.

Let's take a look at how we can break up the rigidity of our grid by moving a few elements out of alignment. Say we have a 20-pixel gap between each container box on our page. We can use measurements like this to maintain consistency, even when we place elements in a grid. In Figure 5.10, you can see that although the box containing the logo has been moved out to the left of the grid that contains the page layout, the extra 20 pixels creates a pleasing consistency with the other elements on the page.

---

[9] http://960.gs/

[10] http://developer.yahoo.com/yui/grids/

[11] http://www.blueprintcss.org/

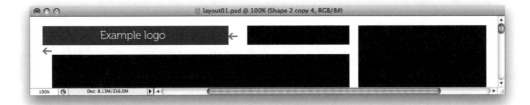

Figure 5.10. Moving the logo out ...

This can be improved, however. Moving the logo out to the left has left a larger gap on the right-hand side. In order to rectify this, let's increase the size of the logo box so that it fills the original space plus the extra 20 pixels needed, as demonstrated in Figure 5.11:

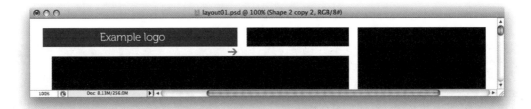

Figure 5.11. ... then adjusting the gap

This shows us that even when breaking out of the grid, we're still using consistent values for how far we push the items out, retaining some uniformity in the layout. We'll use some of these techniques when we put our final design together.

The Artistic Layer

We designers all like to believe we're artists, don't we? Is design art? Perhaps the answer may well be a book all in itself!

Personally, I do design for the same reason I picked up crayons as a toddler and scrawled a multi-colored mess on paper and labelled it "mummy". I'm still on a mission to make stuff look pretty, as you well know. I've moved on from using crayons (they always broke, after all) but other than that, very little has changed.

When you've settled on some ideas for layout and structure, it's time to start thinking about color, imagery, type, and texture—the elements that make our design shine.

Mood and Atmosphere

Overarching all our decisions about color or type is the idea of what mood we want to convey. The mood of our design should reflect the goals of the site and the content within it. As Jeffrey Zeldman writes,[12] "Good web design is about the character of the content, (rather than) the character of the designer."

Mood and atmosphere work on a subconscious level. There's a lack of hard and fast rules about which combination of elements creates which feelings—rather, you'll know when you see it. It's fair to say, though, that mood is most strongly influenced by the artistic decisions you make about your design.

In Figure 5.12, the Johnny Hollow site[13] exudes a dark, gothic atmosphere in line with the band's music and perceived image. This is due to the combination of dark colors, the typography, and the imagery. Contrast this to A Tennessee Winter,[14] shown in Figure 5.13; the site is still atmospheric, but in a completely different way—light in tone, with the use of ice blue and Christmas images to evoke the *feeling* of winter.

In each case, the mood of the site reflects the content.

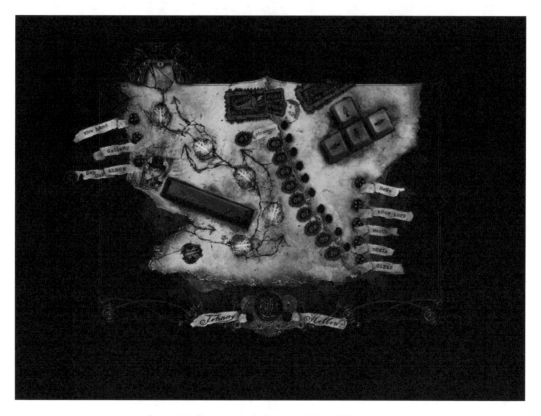

Figure 5.12. Compare the dark, moody Johnny Hollow site ...

---

[12] http://zeldman.com/
[13] http://johnnyhollow.com/
[14] http://winter.tnvacation.com/

Figure 5.13. ... with the soft, wintry tone of the Winter in Tennessee site

We'll want the Web in the Wild site to *feel* like the event itself, and if you think back to the brief we read in Chapter 2, this was specifically requested by our client. The event is about information and knowledge-sharing, so in that sense the site should convey a sense of authority. But it also needs to appear fun, as that's a large part of what the event is also about ... especially with the after-party!

As we work through the process of choosing color, type, and imagery, we'll be keeping these goals in mind.

Color

Color has one of the strongest influences over the appearance of your design. We can use it to evoke feelings, help establish the brand for a site, and set up a guideline for carrying a theme across the web site and any associated materials.

It's fair to say that, as human beings, we rather enjoy looking at colorful objects, but simply making everything as colorful as possible might result in some unattractive combinations. Make your color choices wisely and you'll see that all colors have the ability to work well in a given scenario. Sites like Brunet-García's[15] demonstrate that even colors commonly avoided by most designers can work

---

[15] http://brunetgarcia.com/

just fine in the right context—as Figure 5.14 shows, their design is effective even with loud colors you might normally steer clear of.

Figure 5.14. Punchy pink and yellow

Color Basics

We'd need an entire book to discuss color theory in detail. Here, we'll just touch on the basics.

The color you see on a computer's monitor is based on the red-green-blue **additive** model, shown in Figure 5.15, because these are the three primary colors of light.

However, to discuss color theory in general, we'll use a more traditional **subtractive** model color wheel like the one in Figure 5.16—this still does a decent job of describing color relationships.

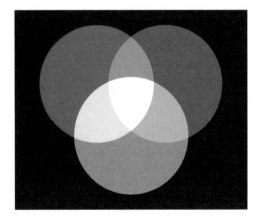

Figure 5.15. The additive color model

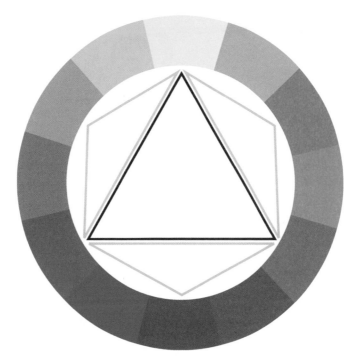

Figure 5.16. A traditional color wheel

One of the goals of color theory is to understand which colors work well together. A color wheel helps us work with **color schemes**—formulas for choosing pleasing color combinations. There are six traditional color schemes:

- **monochromatic**—a single color, and lighter or darker variations of that color

- **analogous**—a group of colors that sit beside each other on the wheel, such as orange, yellow, and green

- **complementary**—colors that are opposite one another on the wheel, such as blue and orange

- **split complementary**—one color, and two colors adjacent to its complementary color

- **triadic**—three colors, equal distances apart

- **tetradic**, or **double complementary**—four colors selected at equal distances, which just happens to create two complementary color schemes

You can see examples of each in Figure 5.17.

Figure 5.17. Left to right: monochromatic, analogous, complementary, split complementary, triadic, and tetradic color selections

Mark Boulton presents some very solid information about color theory in his new book, *A Practical Guide to Designing for the Web*, available as a PDF.[16] I'll recommend again that you head in the direction of Jason Beaird's book, *The Principles of Beautiful Web Design*, for even more detail.

One thing to keep in mind, though, is that despite all the science, we're creating something to please our eyes. Experiment with other combinations. If your eyes feel happy, then go for it!

Color Scheme Inspiration

While an appreciation of color theory will stand you in good stead in placing harmonious colors together, it can be hard to find color inspiration, even for the most experienced designer.

Fortunately, there are plenty of tools to help. The Color Scheme Generator 2,[17] shown in Figure 5.18, is especially helpful—it allows you to alter everything to the *n*th degree in order to find a suitable scheme, and its interface will also teach you a bit about color theory in the process!

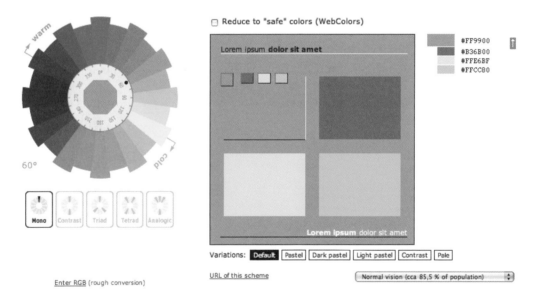

Figure 5.18. The Color Scheme Generator in action

---

[16] http://fivesimplesteps.co.uk
[17] http://www.wellstyled.com/tools/colorscheme2/

Adobe's Kuler[18], seen in Figure 5.19, is even more advanced. It's a Flash-based web application that allows you to browse color schemes from other users, edit color values to your liking, save them for others to find, and export as Adobe color swatch files. Its editor also includes a handy visual wheel to help understand the color schemes we discussed earlier.

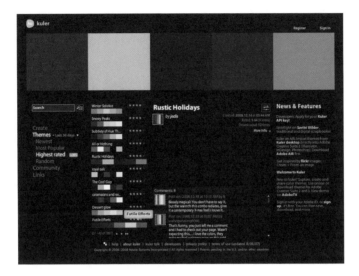

Figure 5.19. Kuler

Another great way to find new color combinations is to visit COLOURlovers,[19] where a similar community-led approach is taken.

Patrick McNeill released a great book called *The Web Designer's Idea Book*[20] (Cincinnati: How Books, 2008), which groups web sites into dominant colors (mainly pink web sites, mainly blue web sites, and so on). This is extremely useful to browse through if you're looking at how other designers have tackled color, especially if you're tied to using one particular scheme for brand consistency.

Knowledgebase, the fictional company hosting our event, has a logo you can see in Figure 5.20—but we're operating without real brand guidelines in terms of color, so we'll have free rein in that respect.

Brought to you by **knowledgebase**

Figure 5.20. The Knowledgebase logo

---

[18] http://kuler.adobe.com/
[19] http://colourlovers.com/
[20] http://amazon.co.uk/dp/1600610641/

Contrast

When designing a web site, it's important that some elements stand out more than others or, to put it more accurately, that there's a hierarchy of what stands out the most right down to what stands out the least. This is an essential part of improving accessibility on a site, since contrast allows a user to easily scan the page for the information they're after. If all elements had an equal weight (and therefore low contrast), it'd be much harder to separate each one, let alone find what you're looking for.

Often contrast will be implied by the physical size of certain elements or their placement on screen, but it's also implied by color.

It's a technique rarely employed, but one way of checking the contrast of your design is to turn your Photoshop document into grayscale. A simple way to do this (to save you actually altering the colors in your document every time) is to create an **Adjustment Layer** above all of your other layers. From the **Layer** menu, select **New Adjustment Layer**, and then **Hue/Saturation**. Now, take the **Saturation** slider right down to 0 and you'll see your document in black and white.

This is only a rough indication of actual contrast, but it does offer you a different perspective on your design, allowing you to step back from creating contrast with color alone.

Consistency

Keeping a consistent, unified theme across your site reinforces your brand, and helps make your site memorable and usable. Repeated themes, using color or type, build a sense of unity about the design, which in turn evokes an almost subliminal sense of comfort.

When working with existing brands, it's inevitable that brand guidelines will exist, to which we must adhere. Even if there's a paucity of formal brand documentation, there will almost certainly be certain stylistic elements a new design ought to inherit. These might include logos, color schemes, graphical elements, or typography.

Even if brand consistency is irrelevant in your circumstances, you'll still need to establish your own guidelines and ensure that a uniformity is maintained across each of the pages.

Volume and Depth

In general, web sites appear to sit on a two-dimensional plane and we use metaphors from the real world to simulate depth, to a degree. At its simplest level, this includes graphical elements such as shadows.

Some designers are more ambitious in their efforts to simulate *real life* depth effects. On ClearLeft's web site for their application Silverback,[21] Paul Annett used several layers of jungle vine graphics to suggest depth, with the nearest ones being out of focus. Then he added some clever CSS to cause the vines to move with the resizing of the browser window, called a **parallax** effect. This describes the way objects closer to us appear to move faster than those in the distance. You can see this in Figure 5.21, although I recommend you view it in a browser to appreciate the full effect!

Figure 5.21. The parallax effect on the Silverback site

But why use techniques such as this? Making a web site realistic may be unsuccessful at improving it: the correlation between depth effects and user satisfaction can fall well short of the mark. However, small touches like the parallax effect can—because of their novelty—engage the user, allowing them to play with a site and therefore enjoy it.

This is a concept we see lots of in Flash-based sites, and sadly very little of in the world of HTML and CSS.

Pattern and Texture

I'm rather fond of patterns and texture—they add a more interesting element to what would otherwise be flat areas of color. They also add a sense of reality to a design, breaking up harsh technological blandness and reminding us of tangible, real life objects. A previous design on Tim van Damme's site Maxvoltar,[22] shown in Figure 5.22, evoked the feeling of a letterpressed card by combining type and color with a subtle paper texture.

Figure 5.22. Maxvoltar's use of type, color, and papery texture[23]

Texture also plays a major role with various interface elements. Think of the *button* look that makes an item seem clickable, or the same effect with depressed styling, so that it looks like it's been pressed in or selected. By employing textures similar to those found in real life, it's easier for users to grasp the function of these elements. Another example would be the lines on a draggable component, such as the slider control shown in Figure 5.23. It appears as if the item could be gripped.

Figure 5.23. Grab onto this!

---

[22] http://maxvoltar.com/
[23] This design is no longer online.

Imagery

In Chapter 1 we briefly discussed the two types of images used in web design: content-based images, and those purely presentational. To clarify, a content image could be a photo used to illustrate a newspaper article, or a picture of a house used on a property-finding web site. A presentational image might be a rounded corner graphic used on a navigation bar, or a repeated pattern used for the main web site background.

Photography

Figure 5.24. A large photograph forms the background of a FOWA design[24]

In the early days of the Web, photography was used sparingly because of the relatively large file sizes associated with images of a decent quality. Luckily, as broadband connections have sped up, we designers can afford the luxury of pushing bigger image files down the pipe. I'm rather fond of large photographic background images, as you can see in Figure 5.24, above.

As viewports grow larger, we have more chances to create bigger background images. Although we still have to consider the size of the viewport, just as we do when designing the main site layout, we have a bit more freedom with the background image; since it serves a purely decorative purpose, it's unimportant if some of the image is clipped by the edge of the window.

---

[24] This design is no longer online.

When a user sees a photograph, they see a recognizable representation of the real world. While this may sound like an obvious thing to say, it's important to establish this connection—especially when describing a situation that occurs offline, such as an event. Images from real life make it easy for the web site's visitors to identify with the design.

Of course, your photos should be appropriate to the mood you'd like to convey with your design. In Figure 5.25, we can see an example of well-chosen imagery from an Alzheimer's self-test site. It's upbeat and positive, showing a professional-looking doctor and happy-looking individuals representing the target audience.

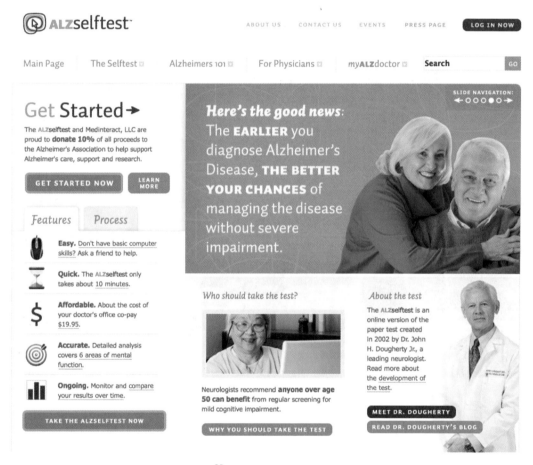

Figure 5.25. ALZselftest[25] keeps it confident, positive, and professional

When it's time for us to include photos in our design, we'll need to keep in mind the brand values *fun* and *informative* that our client asked us to work with. Photographs of people having a great time at a party or as interested audience members would work well for our project—our potential attendees could picture themselves in that situation.

---

[25] http://alzselftest.com/

Beautiful photography is an enormous topic—here are just a few major things to consider when choosing images:

1. Be sure to make some Levels and Curves adjustments to the photo if the shot requires it (and it almost always does!). For example, a yellow cast from tungsten lighting can make the entire photograph look murky. For a tutorial on how to use the Photoshop Levels tool, check out this tutorial from Creative Pro magazine.[26]

2. A shallow depth of field can be a great way to allow the subject to stand out from the background, and remove any distractions. You can achieve this by exploring the aperture options on your camera—a wide aperture creates a shallow depth of field, while a narrow aperture keeps more of the photo in crisp focus. You'll find an introduction to these principles at Picture Correct.[27]

3. Try to avoid blurry photos, unless the blur is intentional. You might want to creatively use blur to imply movement or action. For some inspiration, see the Digital Photography School blog's 15 examples of effective deliberate blur.[28]

4. Crop creatively. The focus of a photo can be dramatically altered by adjusting the dimensions of the frame. Mark Boulton wrote an interesting introduction to this at 24ways.[29]

Illustration

Over the last few years, many designers have expressed their distaste for the digitally-led web design aesthetic of yore by including more illustrative imagery as part of their designs. This could include anything like handwritten typography to page elements that look like they were drawn by hand and lack some of the precise dimensions usually associated with web design. On the Joyent[30] site, shown in Figure 5.26, the illustrated characters help to add some interest to the the otherwise dry and technical topic of web hosting.

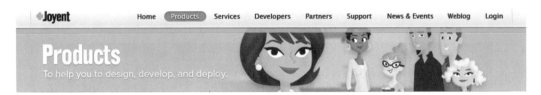

Figure 5.26. The Joyent web site's illustrated figures

---

[26] http://www.creativepro.com/article/advanced-color-correction-with-photoshop-levels/

[27] http://www.picturecorrect.com/photographytips/208/aperture_fstops_camera_settings.htm

[28] http://digital-photography-school.com/blog/blur-movement/

[29] http://24ways.org/2008/art-directing-with-looking-room/

[30] http://joyent.com/

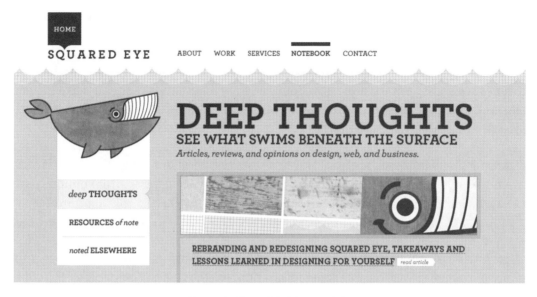

Figure 5.27. Squared Eye's happy whale

However, the term illustration goes beyond describing graphics that look like they're made by hand. It may refer to imagery that references both the written content and informs the actual page layout, such as the smiling whale found on the Squared Eye web site.[31] In the example in Figure 5.27, you can see how the whale dominates and affects the navigation on the left-hand side—a dramatic and interesting way to highlight that area.

Iconography

Iconography falls somewhere between the two categories of content and presentation. Icons could be seen as presentational because sometimes all they do is enhance the text's meaning.

On Raka Creative's[32] homepage, the icons beside each heading add some visual interest, as you can see in Figure 5.28.

Figure 5.28. A section of the Raka Creative homepage

---

[31] http://squaredeye.com/
[32] http://rakacreative.com/

Sometimes, they can act as content, where an icon is used to completely replace text. On the t-shirt site Threadless,[33] the user is invited to *share* their t-shirts on their favorite social network. As seen in Figure 5.29, the social media service icons are familiar enough to users to convey meaning alone, without needing to list their names as well.

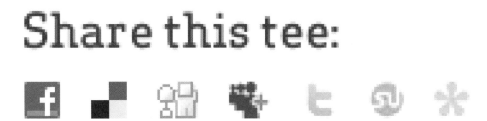

Figure 5.29. Threadless's social media buttons

Image Treatments

Images can be placed into a web page on their own, but that's not really what we're here to do, is it? Even the most basic styling will add a little pizazz.

Basic Borders

Let's imagine an image placed on the page, totally devoid of styling, as in Figure 5.30.

Figure 5.30. An undecorated image

It's fairly uninteresting, would you say? How about we add the very simplest of styles: a black border, one pixel wide? We can see how that would look in Figure 5.31.

[33] http://threadless.com/

Figure 5.31. A thin border adds some minimal definition

That's an improvement. The border adds a slightly more professional look, since the image style has at least been given some thought, but let's continue in this vein and make it more striking. We'll add a white inner border, and then, to really lift the image from the page, simulate a bit of depth by creating a shadow that will sit beneath the frame. Figure 5.32 shows us the final result.

Figure 5.32. That's better!

Advanced Borders

On his tutorial web site, Web Designer Wall, Nick La posted a guide[34] on how to create more interesting, graphically-enhanced borders. As shown in Figure 5.33, these include rough-edged frames and pieces of tape to give a more realistic feel.

Figure 5.33. Different border styles from Web Designer Wall

Typography

A lot of what we'll talk about here refers to techniques we'd implement in the build stage, using CSS, JavaScript, and Flash; you might, therefore, be forgiven for thinking that these considerations are irrelevant to us at the design stage. However, I'm afraid that's far from the case. Today, typography on the Web is the easiest to accomplish it's ever been from a technological perspective, although techniques for doing so can be some of the most technologically challenging to implement. We'll have to take these considerations on during the design process, otherwise we run the risk of designing a site that is impossible (or at least unnecessarily difficult) to build.

---

[34] http://www.webdesignerwall.com/tutorials/css-decorative-gallery/

Type on the Web

In earlier days the only methods we had for displaying type were to either put up with the limited collection of **web-safe fonts**—that is, fonts installed on most operating systems by default—or to make images of text and place these into the document. Now, new standards and techniques are developing that are slowly bringing our control over type one step closer to the world of print design. Knowing which method to use can be a challenge in itself, though, so let's examine the options we have.

Web-safe Fonts

At first glance, our typographic palette seems somewhat limited. There are a number of fonts considered web-safe—that is, reasonably common in many browsers, such as Palatino Linotype, Times New Roman, or Courier New.

Restrictions, restrictions, restrictions! It's far from easy being a web designer, but we can still be creative. When fonts are specified in a cascading style sheet, it's possible to list as many fonts as you like in a **font stack**—a set of font names ordered from most to least preferred. Many fonts are packaged with popular software applications, such as Adobe Creative Suite or Microsoft Office, and we're able to use these as well to provide enhanced typography for those users who happen to have them installed. The last option from the list—usually a generic font family declaration, like cursive or sans-serif—is displayed for those users without these fonts. For a discussion of relatively common fonts that can be used, take a look at Eight Definitive Font Stacks[35] on SitePoint—the article discusses eight groups of fonts to use that build on the web-safe choices.

Replacement Technique: Images

An extremely popular way of rendering the text exactly the way you want it is to embed that text into an image. There are a variety of methods for handling image replacement, with the most common being The Phark Revisited method, whereby the text remains in the HTML, but is pushed off screen and the element is assigned a background-image value. Dave Shea detailed this technique and many others on his post Revised Image Replacement.[36]

Replacement Technique: sIFR

A slightly more resilient approach is that of **sIFR,**[37] or scalable Inman Flash Replacement, a technique whereby the HTML text is replaced with Flash text composed of any font you choose.[38] It's great from an accessibility point of view because, like image replacement, the text is right there in the HTML, and simply appears as ordinary text if the user has Flash or JavaScript disabled.

---

[35] http://www.sitepoint.com/article/eight-definitive-font-stacks/

[36] http://mezzoblue.com/tests/revised-image-replacement/

[37] http://mikeindustries.com/blog/sifr/

[38] sIFR is named for Shaun Inman—http://shauninman.com—who pioneered the original Inman Flash replacement method.

Figure 5.34 shows the sIFR demonstration page with Flash on and off—you can see how the text is still meaningful, if less decorative.

Figure 5.34. The sIFR demonstration page using Flash (left) and without Flash (right)

Even though sIFR is a great tool, it can be tricky to implement, which puts many designers off. It's relatively painless, though, and if you're feeling daunted, it's worth checking out sIFR Lite[39] for a potentially easier replacement.

The Argument for Image Replacement

In case you're wondering why I'm encouraging you to use image replacement instead of just throwing an `img` HTML element in there, it's because it's a wiser choice from an accessibility point of view. It means we can still have the text itself rendered in the HTML, instead of it being potentially lost in an `img` element. It also makes it much easier to maintain, as—like CSS—it separates the content and presentation layers.

The main downside to image replacement centers around accessibility: with images turned off, your titles (or whatever it is you've replaced) completely disappear. Some **screen readers**—tools used by the visually impaired to read aloud text on a screen—will include the text but behavior is inconsistent, even though the text remains embedded in the markup.

For more information on this topic, be sure to check out the CSS-Discuss page on screen reader visibility.[40]

---

[39] http://www.allcrunchy.com/Web_Stuff/sIFR_lite/

[40] http://css-discuss.incutio.com/?page=ScreenreaderVisibility

Font Embedding

A relatively new option to arrive on the scene is the ability to embed font files with your site, which is available to browsers that support this part of the CSS specification: recent versions of Opera, WebKit-based browsers like Safari, and Firefox, as well as Internet Explorer. Since Internet Explorer's favored file format (EOT) is proprietary, it may raise some cross-browser issues; but if you're willing to work around that, it will prove to be a useful tool in the future. For an in-depth discussion of this technique, Jon Tangerine covers the issues in @font-face in IE: Making Web Fonts Work.[41]

Other Methods

Of course, there are plenty of ways to make image replacements. Many other versions of text replacement exist and each one has its own pros and cons, so be sure to investigate your options, experiment with whichever suits you best, and choose the technique that causes the least pitfalls for your intended userbase.

Choosing Typefaces

Fonts, fonts, so many fonts. Now that you're familiar with the various ways we have at our disposal for setting type in a variety of fonts, it's time to make some informed, sensible decisions.

In other words, we need to set everything in Comic Sans.

Okay, just kidding.

You see, fonts have personalities. Comic Sans, as reviled as it is, makes its appearance when someone wants something lighthearted and casual; you'll see an example in Figure 5.35. It's rare to find a serious designer who'll use it, but the principle still stands.

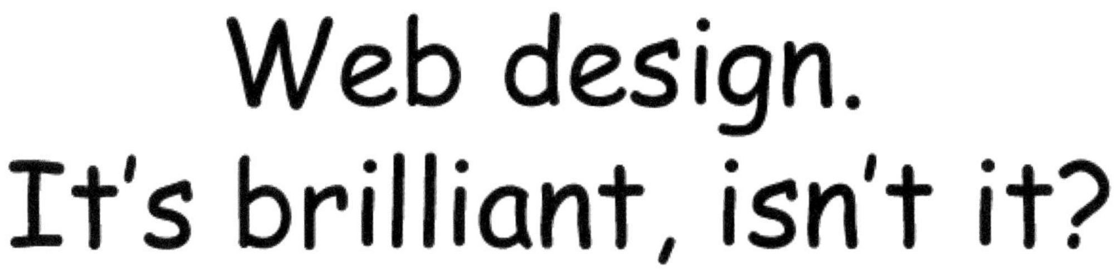

Web design.
It's brilliant, isn't it?

Figure 5.35. Comic Sans in action

Consider the difference between Comic Sans and Times New Roman (Figure 5.36), a font that exudes authority and a serious tone. Yes, it's like newspaper type! That's because it was invented for *The Times* newspaper in London.

---

[41] http://jontangerine.com/log/2008/10/font-face-in-ie-making-web-fonts-work/

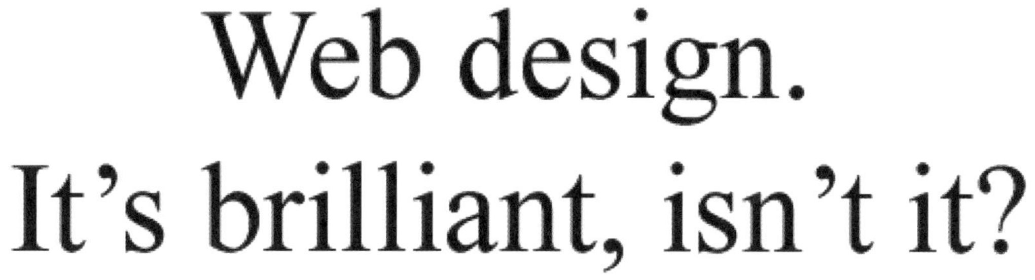

Web design.
It's brilliant, isn't it?

Figure 5.36. Times New Roman font

A typeface like DIN—an uncommon font that falls short of being web-safe—has a sense of authority, but in a different way to Times New Roman. DIN is like a bold statement, unafraid of making a point. As with people, typefaces have different sides to their personalities!

Web design.
It's brilliant, isn't it?

Figure 5.37. The DIN typeface

Decorative Type

In Figure 5.38, Figure 5.39, and Figure 5.40, you can see examples of decorative text used creatively. The SimpleBits site[42] is famous for fancy ampersands; I Love Typography[43] spices up the appearance of post metadata; and designr.it[44] makes extensive use of decorative drop caps.

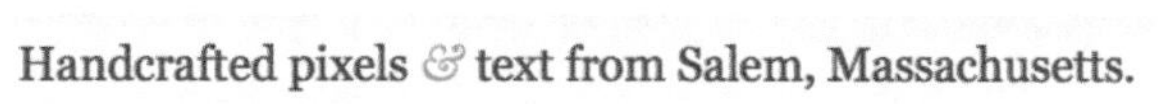

Handcrafted pixels & text from Salem, Massachusetts.

Figure 5.38. Decorative ampersands at SimpleBits

---

[42] http://simplebits.com/
[43] http://ilovetypography.com/
[44] http://designr.it/

{23 comments}

Figure 5.39. Spicy comments at I Love Typography

Figure 5.40. Drop caps at designr.it

Convention versus Innovation

If there is anything I like to make my fellow web designers think about, it is our responsibility to innovate. Every day I catch up with new sites being launched, clicking on an inexhaustible stream of inspiration gallery sites, and every day I'm faced with clone after clone after clone.

We have the power to change this. We're creative people, so let's use our creative powers to push boundaries and experiment with this exciting new technology we have in our hands.

However, as I said back in Chapter 1, even the most creative, original designer in the world should be aware of convention, because it offers us a framework in which to work. But it's an unrestrictive framework: it's one that's based upon tried and tested concepts, fundamentals of web design that users find beneficial.

So each time it comes to designing a new site, we're tasked with finding a balance between convention and innovation. Most of the time it's easy to fall into the comforting cradle of convention and use the safe option, but it's perfectly possible to use convention as a base and then build upon that with a few novel uses of composition, type, color, and the like to make a more interesting experience for your visitors.

Watch Out for That Web 2.0 Look

Some techniques are more popular at the moment thanks to the fad of Web 2.0 design—such as rounded corners on boxes, glassy reflections on logos, punchy colors, or giant fonts. Use with caution!

In November 2007, I did a presentation at the Future of Web Design event in New York called *Destroy The Web 2.0 Look.*[45] In the talk, I was examining how some of these stylistic approaches associated with so-called Web 2.0 sites had wrongly become labelled as the Web 2.0 look. That was the first problem. The second was that, whether good or bad, this aesthetic had become grossly overused because it was mistaken for good web design.

Luckily, since then, we've seen fewer sites blindly adopting that look, and the excessive use of logo reflections and gradients has slowly started to fade.

One thing that remains, however, is the use of so-called Web 2.0 colors. Typically these are vibrant and bold, and often border on the luminous. If you're going to be vibrant, do it tastefully, do it sparingly, and most of all: only do it if it's absolutely necessary!

Putting It All Together

Now that we have some ideas about our design options, it's time to put it all together.

As liberating as a blank canvas can be, it can also be extremely daunting. Where do we start? Where do we place our first mark? Well, the answer is … wherever you feel comfortable. For my part, the starting point in terms of the actual design usually begins with the placement of the logo and branding; then I allow the rest of the design to evolve around it, using my sketches and wireframes as a reference.

Ultimately, design stands apart from science, and although I do think that plans and processes help to keep our work structured, the aesthetics stage should evolve out of experimentation and—importantly—making mistakes. If it fails to work, it can always be changed before you put out the final design. One thing is vital: if it's difficult to make certain elements work with the overall concept, have the courage to let them go. Initially I'd designed a light beige site, seen in Figure 5.41; it had a nice texture, but it lacked any strength, so it had to go.

---

[45] http://elliotjaystocks.com/blog/archive/2007/destroy-the-web-20-look-future-of-web-design-new-york/

Figure 5.41. Fairly nice, but missing that spark

Eventually, I came up with a stronger concept.

The Final Comps

Let's take a look at the final page mockups, shown in Figure 5.42 through to Figure 5.46. We'll look at the aesthetic principles we've been discussing in this chapter, and I'll show you how I put each into practice with these designs.

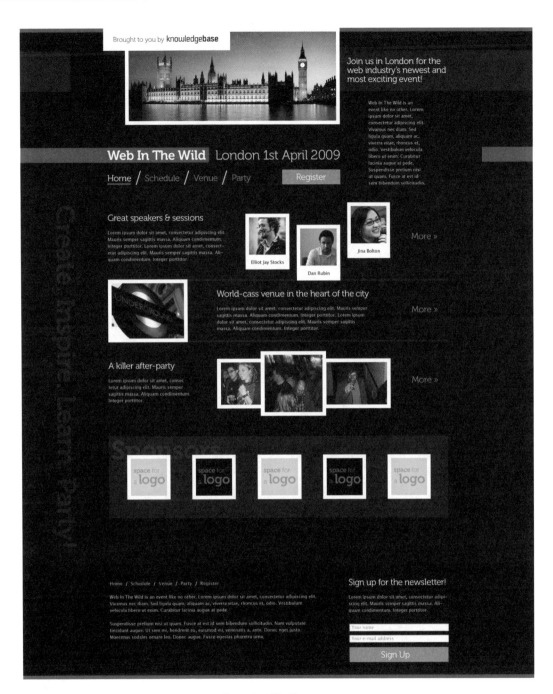

Figure 5.42. The Home page

Figure 5.43. The Schedule page, showing a speaker detail

Figure 5.44. The Venue page

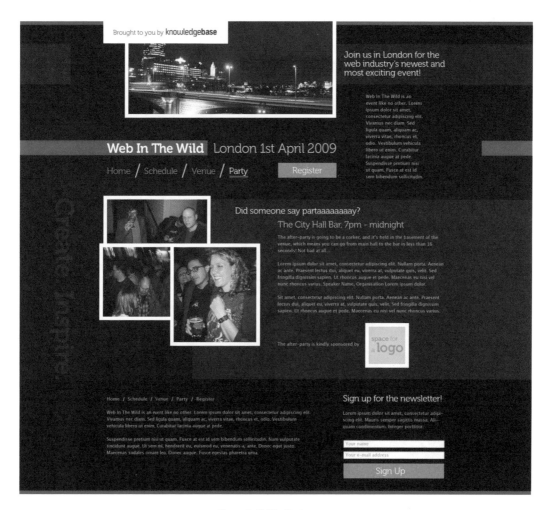

Figure 5.45. The Party page

Figure 5.46. The Register page

Using the Grid

Using our existing wireframes as a reference point, I started by turning these into something more solid and focused, and then looked at ways to break out of the grid.

We already have a set of guides in a Photoshop template from the 960 Grid System to use. It's best not to be afraid of the wireframes or guides, and see them as completely prescriptive: of course, we can use them as a helping hand with our work, but if it's clear that some things would work better if the layout changed, that's fine too. You can see an example of this in Figure 5.47—I've deliberately misaligned some parts of the design, like the photo, tag line and logo that form the header —it makes for a great way to add some breathing space to that part of the layout. Yet it conforms to the grid in terms of how each item has been moved away, so there's still a sense of rhythm and proportion.

Figure 5.47. Consistency is maintained, even though elements appear misaligned

Color

The palette of the site is quite dark, with low-saturation blues forming the main background colors; blue often connotes as being strong and authoritative. This is punctuated with a high-contrast pink (fun, but controversial—it's a bit of a Web 2.0 color!) for the main elements, and a high-contrast blue for hyperlinks.

For a bit of tonal variation to the scheme, I've added two colors for text: an approximate inversion of the dark blue that results in a light beige (tweaked so that the contrast with the background is balanced), and a light teal for additional body text.

On top of this is a generous burst of white here and there, used on the important text to bring the images out with well-defined borders.

Figure 5.48. Color palette for our site

Imagery

In this design we're going to keep it relatively simple when it comes to image treatments, adding a few subtle style elements to maintain some visual interest. There are only two things to note about the way I've handled inline images: they have a 10-pixel border, and their placement is designed to sit slightly outside the flow of content—again, while still conforming to the grid. On the Home and Party pages, images are intentionally misaligned to create a more *fun* atmosphere (although they still only break away by 20 pixels, thus maintaining a harmony of sorts). Figure 5.49 shows us this treatment on some of the photos from the homepage.

Figure 5.49. Intentionally uneven placement adds interest

In the end, I decided to keep the image treatments minimal. I originally experimented with an additional outer border, but it seemed unnecessary, when the rest of the site utilized thick, bold lines. It was for the same reason that I decided to forego other embellishments such as shadows: it overcomplicated the design.

I've also created some basic icons for the travel information shown on the Venue page, which you can see in Figure 5.50:

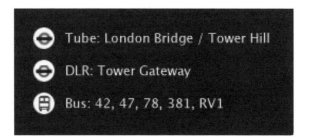

Figure 5.50. Travel icons

Patterns and Texture

The entire design has a layer of subtle **noise** that stops the background colors from appearing flat. Noise adds a film-like grain to an image, which in this design is complemented by the photograph of the building. The image is so low in contrast and treated to blend in well as a background that it effectively becomes a texture in itself. It also reinforces the London theme by using a photo of the venue. Here's the texture in detail, in Figure 5.51.

Figure 5.51. This semi-transparent photograph overlays the blue background

Contrast and Emphasis

In addition to the contrast created by the colors, large blocks of solid color help to separate each element, such as the session and speaker details shown in Figure 5.52. The images are brought out from the background by bold white borders, and each page swaps between the formal structure of content contained within blocks to content placed outside of them; this is made even clearer by the contrast between background and text.

Our color choices can also help to establish a hierarchy of important information—for example, we can reduce the contrast of text slightly as it lowers in importance.

Figure 5.52. Contrast helps give some definition to the schedule's session column and speaker details

Consistency in Our Design

Our client chose not to impose any brand guidelines in the brief, but our use of design elements should always have a consistent look and feel.

Looking back at each of the mockups, you can see various elements that maintain consistency: the generic styling of images, their placement outside of the main areas, and the consistent color scheme. Even elements that change between pages, such as the London image at the top of every page, has consistency, since its placement on each page remains the same.

Our Use of Type

Big, bold headings are the name of the game on our web site, and I've set all headings in Museo,[46] a very sexy font, free from Jos Buivenga.

To achieve the exact effect we'd like to see in our type, I'll suggest we use some image replacement when it comes to the build stage. A potential problem with this method is that these image-based headings are unable to resize along with the text, but since our heading text is quite large and legible already, it's less of an issue.

The event's goals—create, inspire, learn, and party—are rendered as part of the background image, sitting off to the left of the content as an enhancement for users with larger viewports. I felt it was unnecessary to have that text in the main area, however its inclusion as a faux sidebar—and its 90° rotation—adds an interesting element to the design.

Our Use of Convention and Innovation

With a grid system in place and elements that snap directly into its boundaries, our design might be in danger of seeming boring. But the variation we've achieved within the grid—and the layout

---

[46] http://www.josbuivenga.demon.nl/museo.html

that appears to nudge elements out of their parent containers—should catch the eye of a potential attendee.

We've made sure to emphasize all the right elements and keep everything legible, clear, and pleasing to the eye. But a bold color scheme, a large branding area above the main logo, and a layout that appears to *think outside the box* means that we can show our love of experimentation within the confines of tried-and-tested web design conventions.

With both convention and innovation in abundance, this site will seem reliable enough to warrant some attention from professionals, while also stimulating ideas about forward-thinking and beautiful design, appealing to the audience's inclination towards a design that's a bit special.

Conclusion

There's no one universal truth to creating an aesthetically pleasing web site—or indeed an artifact of any kind—but by following the guidelines outlined in this chapter, you'll certainly be on your way! Thanks to the work of scientists and artists spanning thousands of years, we have frameworks to guide our design process—grid systems that appeal to the human eye, color wheels that explain the way we can combine different hues, and conventions that can be subtly modified to provide some pleasant surprises.

It's easier to create sexy designs when we follow such guidelines; we can push the boundaries of what's acceptable with small bits of experimentation that attract attention.

Our target audience for this site are our peers—that is, other web designers—and that's a great reason to try some techniques that are a bit out of the ordinary. Our design adds some bite to conventional design practice … and that's sexy.

Chapter 6

Deliverables

In Chapter 5, we saw designs for our site taking shape, and in this final chapter our designs will be complete and ready to deliver.

Throughout this chapter I'll be using Adobe Photoshop in these examples. If you use an alternative application, that's still okay—the techniques and processes can be applied to a variety of applications. Many designers like using Adobe Fireworks, which has some tools specifically geared towards web design, such as the ability to save various pages within one document.

As I mentioned back in Chapter 1, it's useful if the persons who design the site are also responsible for building the site, since that ensures an insider view of the design process, allowing the designer to design a site with the development stage in mind. However, this may be impractical, and in many companies (particularly larger ones), the designers and developers will always be separated. Luckily, regardless of whether you're handing over the design to a developer, or handling it all yourself, the deliverable stage remains virtually the same. It's all about moving out of your design tool of choice and preparing to put it into the browser.

This will be examined from two points of view:

- delivery of mockups for client approval
- delivery of images, ready for development

We've been concerning ourselves mostly with the design aspect throughout this book, but as we've also been keeping CSS techniques in mind, we'll take a quick look at how some of them might be put into practice.

Design Comps

Call them comps, call them mockups, call them whatever you like. In this final part of our design process, we'll be preparing our Photoshop files in such a way that they can be shown to the client. In one sense this means exporting flat images for the client to look at and approve, as well as making the Photoshop file as useful as possible for the development stage, regardless of whether we're handing it over to a third party.

Organizing Layers

Keeping your workspace organized is going to make your life infinitely easier for when you're working, naturally, as well as if you have to come back to the files at a much later date and need to remember where you placed certain elements. Naming your layers and sorting them into **Layer Groups**—folders that can contain layers and further subfolders—will also benefit anyone else who has to work with your files. If you're handing over your Photoshop files to another designer or developer, then it really is vital for you to do this.

In Figure 6.1, you can see the **Layers** palette for our main Photoshop file. It contains three main Layer Groups:

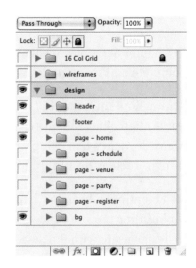

- 16 Col Grid—for the 16-column guides from the 960 Grid System, which we used earlier
- wireframes—for the neater, grid-based layout blocks
- design—for the actual design

Within each of these Layer Groups there are further ones still: within the design Layer Group, there's a general group to contain fixed content that rarely changes (such as the header and footer) and a group for the variable content—that is, the individual pages on the site.

Figure 6.1. Our Layer Groups

Maintaining an organized collection of layers like this keeps your workspace neat, and has a practical use as well. We can show and hide Layer Groups, which makes it easier to *turn off* certain pages when designing. You can see eye icons beside some of these Layer Groups, indicating that they are visible.

Notes

We also have the ability to make notes directly in the Photoshop file by using the **Notes** tool. This is a handy little feature you can use to annotate parts of your design, and it saves trying to describe it to your developer via email! You can see an example of a note in Figure 6.2: I've used it as a reminder of which photo file to use.

Notes are invisible when the document is saved or printed, so it's okay to leave these wherever you like, or delete as you see fit.

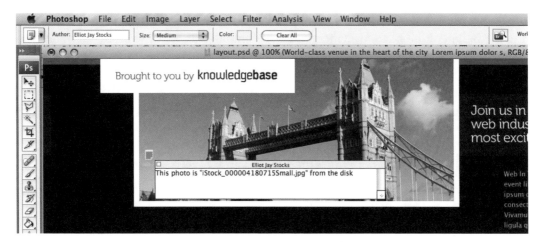

Figure 6.2. A Note about a header photo

Exporting Our Images

Using well-organized layers is helpful when it's time to export images—both full-size mockups and individual parts of the design.

Exporting Mockups

The Layer Groups we mentioned earlier make it easy to export mockups for the client to see, since turning whole pages on and off can be done in an instant.

In our Photoshop file, we have a Layer Group for each of the five pages, and by hiding and showing these Groups, you can quickly and easily export various pages. To export each mockup as cleanly as possible, simply turn off all the layers that belong to another page. Looking back at Figure 6.1, you can see the header, footer, background (marked here as "bg"), and assorted home groups are evident—with these switched on, it's easy to export the homepage mockup.

Exporting Individual Images

Exporting an entire comp is relatively straightforward, but what about exporting individual parts of the design as images, ready to reference in a CSS file? Let's tackle each issue individually.

The Main Background

With its color strips, venue photograph, and grain-like noise, the background of our design has ended up being a rather complex image. This is potentially rather tricky, since we want the textured part of the background to repeat indefinitely (as the width and height of the browser expand), without affecting the image. The grain texture can repeat forever and so can the color. But what about the building image, and the lighter, semi-transparent block that houses the main content? I've isolated these problem areas, as seen in Figure 6.3.

The transparent block has to be treated separately to the page's background image because it has to extend to the height of the content, which could well change depending on the page and the size of the user's text. You see, there are all these considerations we have to keep in mind!

There's another uncertainty we need to account for: if the page is particularly tall, we'd want to avoid the building image and pink blocks repeating down the page. Yikes! It's time to draw up an action plan of the elements we need to separate:

- noise texture: can repeat on both the x (horizontal) and y (vertical) axes
- pink blocks, building photograph, and tag line: can repeat on the x axis only
- semi-transparent content block: must be separated entirely, as its height is constantly variable

Luckily, this is all achievable with minimal fuss (I told you I'd been keeping this stuff in mind!). Here's how we can accomplish everything we want with just three elements and some simple CSS rules:

- noise texture: we'll export this as a simple 100x100px tile, apply it as the `background-image` of the `html` element, and set to repeat on both axes
- pink blocks, building photograph, and tag line: we'll apply this `background-image` to the `body` element and set to repeat on the x axis only
- semi-transparent content block: we can apply this as a `background-image` of a `div` that surrounds the content area, set to repeat on both axes

There we are—all sorted!

Figure 6.3. A troublesome background

Heading Images

As you'll recall from Chapter 3, we'll be recommending to the client that the header graphic text will be included using an image replacement technique. Since the pink bars that form part of the heading are actually a part of the background image applied to the body element, we can leave them out of our header graphics. We can therefore export the main title and subsequent headings for the other pages as semi-transparent **PNGs**—the Portable Network Graphic format, which allows for smooth transparency—cropped to just outside the boundaries of the characters, as in Figure 6.4.

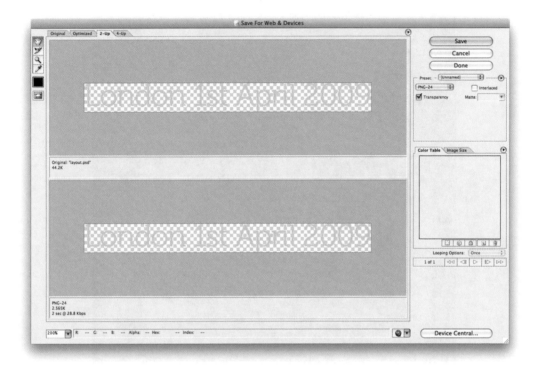

Figure 6.4. Exporting as a PNG preserves the smooth edges

Exported PNGs can be a large file size, however, making it seem slow on the user's end. PNGs can also prove problematic when trying to play nice with older versions of Internet Explorer—IE fails to support PNG's transparency feature at all, and leaves a hideous grey block where your pretty transparent parts should be. There are a couple of different ways to avoid this, but the quickest is by exporting our images as GIFs instead. GIFs support simple transparency, so images saved in this format will have jagged edges. Choose a color from the **Matte** menu that closely matches the background color—as with the lower example in Figure 6.5—and the jagged edges will appear much less prominent when they are displayed on the background.

Figure 6.5. Exporting our header as a GIF

It's all about finding the balance between a flawless appearance, or catering for older browsers!

Navigation Images

Exporting the navigation graphics will be a similar process to exporting the headings, since these buttons will be displayed using the same kind of image replacement technique.

However, there's an extra consideration: if I were to build this site, I'd use a technique called **CSS sprites** to achieve each of the normal, hover, and active states of the buttons. Instead of having to create three separate images for each button, which would create fifteen little images, we'll just use one image with all three states of each button. We'll then use CSS to specify the large image as the background of *every* navigation element, offsetting the position of the background at the right spot to expose the appropriate button. Because the browser only has to download one large image, it means that the user will see the button change instantly, instead of waiting for each of the fifteen images to download.

You can read more about CSS sprites in the A List Apart article *CSS Sprites: Image Slicing's Kiss of Death,*[1] or follow a dedicated tutorial on my own site, called *Better Nav Image Replacement.*[2]

---

[1] http://alistapart.com/articles/sprites/
[2] http://elliotjaystocks.com/blog/archive/2007/css-tutorial-better-nav-image-replacement/

You can see how this would work in terms of how we export the image in Figure 6.6: it almost looks like a table, with each column representing a single button, and each row representing each state. We can employ the same technique to create the order status navigation on the Register page as well.

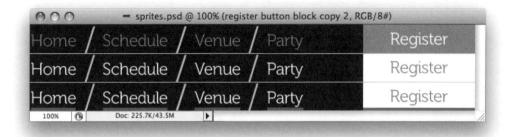

Figure 6.6. The navigation area sprites

Photos

Our photo treatments are fairly straightforward: these will largely be handled by CSS, so there's little to worry about when exporting them from our image editor.

However, the main London-themed image that appears at the top of the site deserves a bit of consideration. A different photo is shown on every page, and it's possible that our client may want to change this image themselves. Potentially it's an awkward shape, as you can see in Figure 6.7—the KnowledgeBase logo appears to cut into the top-left corner, creating an irregular shape.

Figure 6.7. A potentially sticky situation!

The good news is we're able to keep it fairly simple here as well. We'll keep the photos square, and then we'll just use CSS to position a separate image of the KnowledgeBase logo over the top. That way our client's developers can use a regular rectangular image, meaning that they can avoid having to dive into Photoshop to superimpose the logo.

Presenting Mockups in the Browser

To show your client how the design would look in situ, it's advisable to present your design in a browser—because that's the only way to know for sure that it works! Your client will probably also be interested in seeing what appears above **the fold**—that is, the content that can be seen without scrolling. It also means you can test the site out in a variety of resolutions before you even start coding.

One of the mistakes I made regularly in the early stages of my career was presenting the mockups to my clients by attaching them as images to an email. Avoid this at all costs! If you're designing a web site, present it in a browser because—surprise, surprise—that's where we view web sites!

After realizing my mistake I took to uploading images and sending my clients links to them. However, although this was an improvement on sending the mockups via email, it was still far from ideal, because browsers often resize large image files, and creating a horrible white background around smaller ones. The best option is to create a basic HTML template, which is what we'll look at now.

 The Unpredictable Fold

Just as the width of a browser window is unpredictable, so too is the height. While you can have an educated guess at what most people will see without scrolling, there'll always be some people who can see a little more or a little less.

HTML Templates

Creating a template to use as a mockup showcase is very simple indeed. In the text editor of your choice, simply make a file that contains nothing but the shell of a HTML document, with some basic CSS in the `style` element. Specify your page mockup image as the `background-image` of the `body` element, and it will display full-size in the browser.

Here's the markup we'd use to achieve such an effect:

```
<!DOCTYPE html PUBLIC "-//W3C//DTD XHTML 1.0 Strict//EN"
    "http://www.w3.org/TR/xhtml1/DTD/xhtml1-strict.dtd">
<html xmlns="http://www.w3.org/1999/xhtml" lang="en-US">
  <head>
    <title>Homepage Mockup</title>
    <style type="text/css" media="screen, projection">
      * {
        margin: 0;
        padding: 0;
      }

      body {
        height: 2000px;
        width: 1420px;
        background: url(homepage.jpg) top center no-repeat;
      }
    </style>
  </head>
  <body>
    : We can just leave this body area empty
  </body>
</html>
```

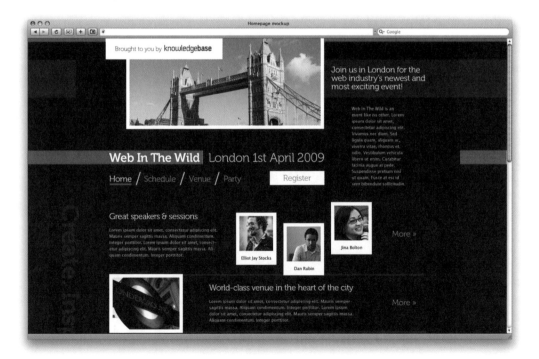

Figure 6.8. Our mockup in the browser

If you have a repeating background pattern and need to show how it would work, simply add that as a background image to the `html` element, like so:

```
html {
  background: url(pattern.jpg);
}
```

Just be sure to remember to change the height and width on the `body` declaration to match the dimensions of your mockup; that way, the browser will expand the `body` element as far as it needs to go, and show scroll bars where necessary. Figure 6.8 shows us how it looks.

Functional Mockups

One step up from a browser-presented mockup is a semi-functional site; that is, a basic HTML (or Flash) site that allows for some limited functionality. The site may still be barely more than an image, but adding some invisible **hit areas**—that is, clickable regions—over the navigation shown in the image could allow the client to see some simple interaction between pages. Here's how you can do it, using some more simple CSS.

First, we'll need to determine the position of each hit area in your mockup. In Photoshop, we can do this using the **View** menu to switch on the **Info** panel.

Next, use the rectangular marquee selection tool to select the region you want to turn into a hit area. The **Info** panel will tell you the width and height of your selection in the area marked W and H. It's a good idea to make a note of that number! In Figure 6.9, I've selected the Register button (I've also switched the guides back on, so it's easier to select the precise area I want to measure). You can see that the **Info** panel is telling me that the area is 160 pixels wide and 40 pixels high.

Finally, we can point the cursor at the top left point of our rectangular selection. The section marked **X:** and **Y:** will tell us the X and Y coordinates of the mouse position. Make a note of those figures too—in this example, the Register button is positioned 720 pixels from the left (X), and 380 pixels from the top (Y).

Figure 6.9. The Info window tells me about the selected Register area

Now, let's head back to the HTML document with our mockup background image. We'll use those figures in a CSS declaration that will position an a element at the right place.

```
<!DOCTYPE html PUBLIC "-//W3C//DTD XHTML 1.0 Strict//EN"
  "http://www.w3.org/TR/xhtml1/DTD/xhtml1-strict.dtd">
<html xmlns="http://www.w3.org/1999/xhtml" lang="en-US">
  <head>
    <title>Homepage Mockup</title>
    <style type="text/css" media="screen, projection">
      * {
          margin: 0;
          padding: 0;
      }

      body {
          height: 2000px;
          width: 1420px;
          background: url(homepages.jpg) top center no-repeat;
      }

      a#register {
          display: block;
          width: 160px;
          height: 40px;
          position: absolute;
          top: 380px;
          left: 720px;
      }
    </style>
  </head>
  <body>
      <a id="register" href="register.html"> </a>
  </body>
</html>
```

Try it out in your web browser. You'll find the Register button is now clickable!

Style Guides

Style guides are one of the most important deliverables of all, as they ensure that anyone else who works on the site after you've handed over your design has a clear idea of color, type, layout, and other pertinent details.

Of course, many styles can be inferred from the design of the site itself, but it's going to be helpful for our client to have a dedicated style guide that details various conventions we've used in our design. It offers unambiguous instructions for how the design is put together, and leaves no room for confusion on the part of another designer or developer.

You can put together a style guide however it seems fit. Some clients would prefer to receive a style guide in the form of a printable document, like a PDF. Others might be happy for you to simply include the instructions as a Layer Group in your file, which is a handy method for keeping the instructions and the materials together.

We'll talk about this briefly, but you can read more on style guides in Jina Bolton's article *Writing an Interface Style Guide*[3] at A List Apart, which includes dozens of comments from other designers and developers.

 Good for Developers

If you're going to develop the site yourself, a style guide is also handy for you—for example, if your client makes contact again in six months and asks you to create some new graphics, you might find it's difficult to remember every detail of how it all fits together!

Layout

We've taken great care to ensure that our layout conforms to a grid, so it's important that any additions to the site follow suit. Be sure to explain the method you used to place elements and lay out your pages, and point out any helpers you might have used—in this example, I'd tell the reader about the 960 Grid System I used and how it works. Because the 960 Grid System comes with a set of CSS styles to assist a developer, they might appreciate the time-saving aspect of this, too.

Color

The exact values for the colors you've used should certainly be defined in your guide. A **color swatch** is essentially a collection of colors used in a design. This graphical representation of the palette can be presented in any way you choose, although an easily recognizable format is as a group of small squares. You can see how I've arranged mine in Figure 6.10.

---

[3] http://www.alistapart.com/articles/writinganinterfacestyleguide/

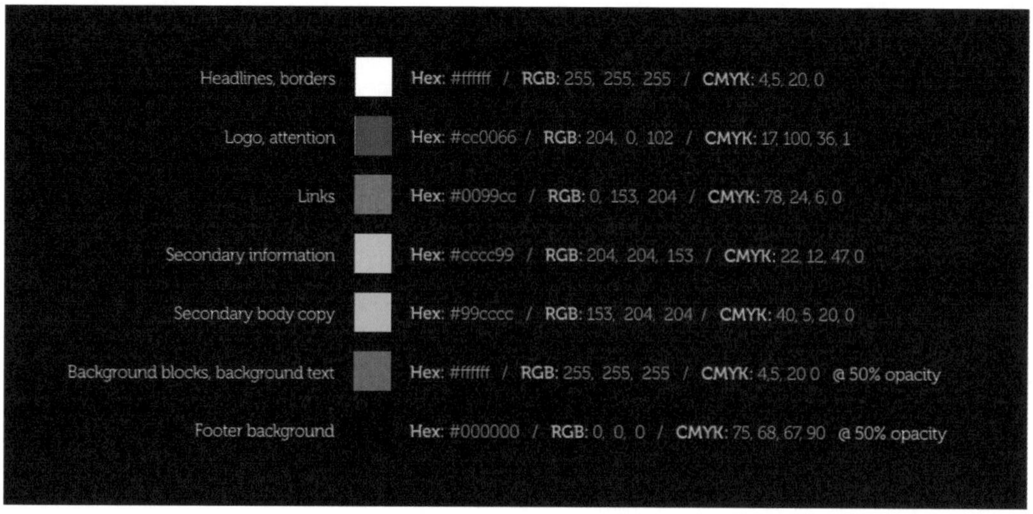

Figure 6.10. A color swatch

When you present your colors as an image, it also makes sense to label them with their corresponding numerical values using a **hexadecimal**, six-character code, **RGB** (for red-green-blue) values, and **CMYK** (cyan-magenta-yellow-key): you'll also see I specified these values back in Figure 6.10. The hexadecimal and RGB values can be used in CSS files, and the CMYK values will help a print designer take the color scheme to use in print documents and match it as closely as possible.

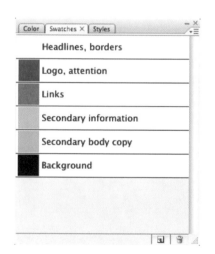

Figure 6.11. Some swatches

In modern image editors it's possible to create and save color swatches, which makes storing and editing them very easy. Adobe have even developed a file format for storing and sharing swatches, and you can open and edit Adobe swatch files in applications such as Photoshop or Illustrator. Figure 6.11 shows an example of the **Swatches** palette, with our design's swatches open. You'll find details on how swatches work in your trusty **Help** menu, but if you'd prefer to be shown, see a video tutorial at TechTutor.tv.[4]

---

[4] http://www.techtutor.tv/photoshop-cs3/use-the-swatches-palette-in-photoshop-cs3.html. This video tutorial is for Photoshop CS3, but the method is still the same for CS4.

Motifs and Techniques

If you've used particular motifs or techniques in your design that should be carried
across to other sites, or if you think there
may be new graphics added later, it's a good
idea to describe in detail how to achieve the
same effect. Be sure to write these down,
and show and tell, if necessary. Photoshop
also allows you to copy and paste layer
styles from one layer to another, which
could be helpful for creating new objects
later. You'll find this option by right-click-
ing a layer and selecting **Layer Style**, shown
in Figure 6.12.

Figure 6.12. Look for the **Layer Style** option when you right-click a layer

Type and Text

The main headings on the site design (to be achieved by image replacement) are set in Museo 300,
with the exceptions being the actual name of the event and the 'Create. Inspire. Learn. Party!' text
in the background, set in the heavier Museo 700. The body text, which is standard HTML, is set in
Lucida Grande—a web-safe font—and a larger font size is used for subheadings. Each detail of these
typographic styles requires explanation; a simple way to do this is to put them in an easy-to-digest
list in the style guide document, as shown in Figure 6.13.

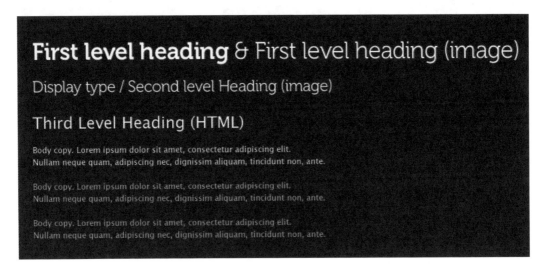

Figure 6.13. Our site's typography, shown by example

If you're using a free font, like we have with Museo, you might want to provide the font files for the developer to use, or at least indicate a place to download it. For licensed fonts, such as the ones that come with Adobe Creative Suite, you might like to let your clients know how and where the font can be purchased.

Images

Our treatment of imagery forms an extremely important part of consistency across the pages in this site. We've already talked about the way all our images have a 10 pixel white border, and how all of our elements, including the images, line up to a grid. This in turn informs the way images should be cropped and resized. We'll need to find a way to convey these guidelines to our developer in our style guide, and again, showing by example is a great way to do this. You can see how I've chosen to do it visually via the annotations shown in Figure 6.14.

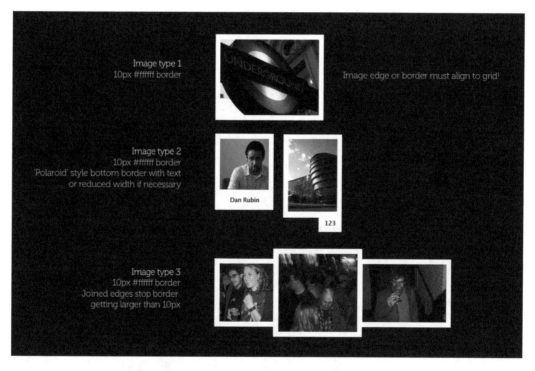

Figure 6.14. Annotated images

Development Matters

With the design for Web in the Wild, we've been keeping mindful of development issues, such as whether the design should be fixed or flexible, image replacement techniques for headings, and using CSS sprites to achieve interesting rollover effects with our navigation elements. Be sure to address these issues in your style guide, so that you and the developer are sure to be on the same page. You might even like to provide links to articles or tutorials detailing the techniques you had in mind when you worked through the design.

Anything Else?

Of course, if there's anything else you need to convey to your client, you should let them know. We've spent a lot of time thinking carefully about the goals of this event and the brand values our client asked us to convey through our design—don't let all that hard work go to waste! Be sure to point out any guidelines you think would be necessary for how to keep the message and the meaning of your design consistent.

What Now?

Whew! We've done so much so far:

- We've done plenty of *research*—helping our client write a brief, and gathering up as much detail about their requirements as we can. With some decent client–designer communication about the project's goals, as well as collecting great design inspiration and ideas, we've built some solid foundations for our design.

- We've thought carefully about *structure*—how the site will eventually be used. We've seen how to sensibly plan a web site's anatomy and work from sketchbook doodles, right through to comprehensive sitemaps and annotated structure diagrams.

- We've examined the various forms of *interaction* that happen on web pages—from top-level navigation down to search forms, multimedia players, and basic ecommerce procedures. With the aim of making everything as simple for the user as possible, we've explored how to grant easy access to any of the information contained on a web site. We've put it all together in a series of wireframes we can use to show our client what we'd like to do, and to give us a solid idea of the final design we'd like to create.

- We've thought of *aesthetics*—adding a layer of beauty that will keep visitors returning time and time again. We've made sure we kept it usable by employing traditional conventions, while gently pushing the boundaries for a sexy and interesting look.

- Finally, we compiled a set of *deliverables* that make it easy for our client and their developers to put it all together into a living, breathing web site.

What's next? It's time to give our client those Photoshop files, the exported images, and the style guide. Then …

Relax! We've just finished a very sexy web design.

Good Luck, You Sexy Thing

So we've reached the end! I hope you've enjoyed the ride, and that you feel you've learned a lot about the process of building a sexy web site.

Hopefully, you now have an idea of how to tackle an in-depth design project, and will approach such a task with a new set of eyes. I trust that some of the techniques discussed in this book have shed new light on common tasks, and that the various web sites I've shown are inspirational.

Although I've tried to present ideas and techniques in a thorough and informative way, my aim has been to provide more than just a straight reference manual. Instead, I hope the ideas from this book act as a source of inspiration—something you can flick through on a rainy day, and find ideas that will breathe new life into your projects for years to come.

There are some very talented designers out there, creating some very sexy designs. I hope this book will enable you to become one of them.

Index

THE ART & SCIENCE OF CSS

BY **CAMERON ADAMS**
JINA BOLTON
DAVID JOHNSON
STEVE SMITH
JONATHAN SNOOK

CREATE INSPIRATIONAL STANDARDS-BASED WEB DESIGN

THE PRINCIPLES OF
BEAUTIFUL
WEB DESIGN

BY JASON BEAIRD

DESIGN BEAUTIFUL WEB SITES USING THIS SIMPLE STEP-BY-STEP GUIDE

SIMPLY
JAVASCRIPT

BY **KEVIN YANK**
& CAMERON ADAMS

THE ULTIMATE

CSS

REFERENCE

Tommy Olsson & Paul O'Brien